DEC Recommended
Practices

DEC Recommended Practices Monograph Series

DEC Recommended Practices:
Enhancing Services for Young Children With Disabilities and Their Families

DEC Recommended Practices

*Enhancing Services for Young Children
With Disabilities and Their Families*

DEC Recommended Practices Monograph Series

Los Angeles

Copyright 2015 by the Division for Early Childhood (DEC) of the Council for Exceptional Children

All rights reserved

No portion of this monograph may be reproduced by any means, electronic or otherwise, without the express written permission of the Division for Early Childhood (DEC) of the Council for Exceptional Children.

ISBN: 978-0-9819327-9-8

Disclaimer

The opinions and information contained in the articles of this monograph are those of the authors of the respective articles and not necessarily those of the Division for Early Childhood (DEC) of the Council for Exceptional Children. Accordingly, DEC assumes no liability or risk that may be incurred as a consequence, directly or indirectly, or the use and application of any of the contents of this monograph.

DEC does not perform due diligence on advertisers, exhibitors, or their products or services and cannot endorse or guarantee that their offerings are suitable and accurate.

Published and Distributed by:

The Division for Early Childhood
3415 S. Sepulveda Blvd. Suite 1100
Los Angeles, CA 90034
Phone: (310) 428-7209

E-mail: dec@dec-sped.org
Website: http://www.dec-sped.org/

The Division for Early Childhood (DEC), a division of the Council for Exceptional Children, is an international membership organization for individuals who work with or on behalf of young children with disabilities and other special needs. Founded in 1973, DEC's mission is to promote policies and advance evidence-based practices that support families and enhance the optimal development of young children who have or are at risk for developmental delays and disabilities. Information about membership and other resources available can be found at www.dec-sped.org

Managing editor: Rosa Milagros Santos, *University of Illinois at Urbana-Champaign*
Technical and copy editor: Kevin Dolan
DEC executive director: Leah Weiner
Cover design: Sarah Jane Boecher
Interior design: Kevin Dolan and Sarah Jane Boecher
Typeset in Warnock Pro, Myriad Pro, and Calibri
Photos provided by iStock

Suggested Citation

Division for Early Childhood. (2015). *DEC recommended practices: Enhancing services for young children with disabilities and their families* (DEC Recommended Practices Monograph Series No. 1). Los Angeles, CA: Author.

TABLE OF CONTENTS

Bridging What We Know Works Well in Research to Our Everyday Practice: A Message From DEC

A History of the DEC Recommended Practices
Mary McLean

Revising the Division for Early Childhood Recommended Practices: When, Who, and How
Patricia Snyder and Betsy Ayankoya

LEADERSHIP
Setting the Course and Steering the Ship
Kathleen Hebbeler

ASSESSMENT
Guiding Principles for Accurate and Efficient Decision Making
Jane Squires

ENVIRONMENT
Improving Access and Participation
Tricia Catalino and Lori E. Meyer

FAMILY
Using the Recommended Practices to Build Parent Competence and Confidence
Carol M. Trivette and Rashida Banerjee

INSTRUCTION
Making the Most of Learning Opportunities
Ilene Schwartz and Juliann Woods

INTERACTION
From Qualities of Interaction to Intervention Practices: Using What Comes Naturally
Jeanette McCollum

99 — TEAMING AND COLLABORATION
Thinking About How as Well as What
Chelsea Guillen and Pam Winton

111 — TRANSITION
Using the Recommended Practices to Support Continuity and Transitions
Beth S. Rous

121 — **Voices From the Field**

125 — RESOURCES WITHIN REASON
Foundational Resources for Each Area of the DEC Recommended Practices
Camille Catlett

133 — PARTICIPANTS
Contributors to Revisions of the 2014 Recommended Practices

135 — **Index**

Download the DEC Recommended Practices
www.dec-sped.org/recommendedpractices

A MESSAGE FROM DEC

Bridging What We Know Works Well in Research to Our Everyday Practice

It has been more than 10 years since the last revision of the DEC Recommended Practices *and* about 23 years since the first set of practices was unveiled to the field. The 2014 version of the DEC Recommended Practices represents the most current knowledge available on evidence-based, high-leverage practices to support young children, birth through age 5, with disabilities and their families. DEC aims to bridge research and practice by highlighting those practices that have been shown through research to result in better outcomes for young children with disabilities, their families, and the professionals who work with them. To ensure that these revised practices are accessed and widely used, the complete listing of the practices may be downloaded for free from the DEC website (www.dec-sped.org). We cannot be more excited to share these revisions to the recommended practices with the field!

DEC Recommended Practices: Enhancing Services for Young Children With Disabilities and Their Families is the first of the new DEC Recommended Practices Monograph Series, which continues DEC's tradition of and commitment to translating research into practice. Each monograph in the DEC Recommended Practices series will include information about the most effective ways to improve learning outcomes and promote the development of young children, birth through age 5, who have, or are at-risk for, developmental delays or disabilities. It will also feature DEC staples such as the Resources Within Reason column and other practical tools for the field.

In This Inaugural Issue

In this first issue of the DEC Recommended Practices Monograph Series, we provide the context for the revised recommended practices. DEC members who were integral in the development of the revised recommended practices were invited to serve as authors for each article in this monograph. They also happen to be some of the movers and shakers in our field who help build the knowledge base for these practices!

We begin this monograph with McLean's historical overview of the recommended practices. She details the work over the years by several hundred individuals who committed their time and knowledge into developing practices that ensure young children with disabilities and their families have the best chances for reaching their potential. Snyder and Ayankoya describe the rigorous iterative process used to revise the practices. They describe the important work of the DEC Recommended Practices Commission that spearheaded the revision process with support from the Early Childhood Technical Assistance Center (ECTA), which is funded by the U.S. Department of Education. The bulk of the monograph features an overview of each of the eight topic strands that make up the 2014 revisions to the recommended practices. The authors for each of the eight topic strands describe the current literature and empirical base related to their respective recommended practice topic. Most importantly, they provide suggestions for implementing the practices to support infants, toddlers, and preschoolers with disabilities and their families in inclusive settings.

Hebbeler's article on Leadership highlights the importance of the need for strong leaders if programs are to effectively implement the recommended practices. She discusses how the role of leaders can directly and critically impact the ability of providers to support children with disabilities and their families. In her article on Assessment, Squires challenges us to examine the authenticity of the images that we see through the lenses we use to determine eligibility, diagnoses, and achievement of milestones. Catalino and Myer's article on Environment features one of the new topic strands under the recommended practices. In their article, they emphasize the powerful impact of both physical and temporal environments on children's development. Trivette and Banerjee describe three important guiding principles for Family practices. They also discuss the current empirical literature upon which current practices are based.

Through several vignettes, Schwartz and Woods demonstrate the different ways providers can effectively implement the recommended practices in a variety of EI/ECSE settings. Interaction is another topic strand that is new to the recommended practices. In her article, McCollum hones in on key characteristics of adult-child interactions that support young children's development and growth. Guillen and Winton remind us that Teaming and Collaboration are key ingredients to effective services. They describe the challenges of teaming and collaboration from defining the terms to the composition of teams. The final topic strand focuses on Transition. Rous describes the critical elements embedded within the revised Transition practices, including the timing and the personnel involved in successful transitions.

Voices From the Field and the Resources Within Reason are regular features in the *Young Exceptional Children* journal, which we carried over to this first issue of the DEC Recommended Practices Monograph Series. Read the responses by practitioners, professional development providers, and higher education faculty when asked to comment on the "utility and importance of the DEC Recommended Practices from their perspective as a potential user of these practices." In her popular column, Resources Within Reason, Catlett highlights "foundational" resources for each topic strand, all of which can be accessed online at no cost to the user.

Ways to Use the Monograph Series

Finally, we offer suggestions to practitioners, researchers, and families on ways they can use this new resource in home, school, and community settings:

Professional development providers can review the recommended practices and incorporate these evidence-based interventions into trainings. By using the DEC Recommended Practices, information shared by professional development providers will align with the newest research regarding interventions for young children with disabilities.

The Work Goes On

The ongoing work on revising the DEC Recommended Practices is largely powered by volunteers from the field. You too can be involved by contacting DEC to learn more about how you can participate.

Practitioners can access comprehensive information for enhancing services for young children with disabilities. Professionals can relate the content to the children and families they work with in the classroom. Vignettes included in this publication highlight the recommend practices in action and are applicable to early interventionists and preschool teachers.

Faculty can use this publication to teach the concepts of the DEC Recommended Practices to aspiring professionals in the field of early intervention and early childhood special education. The DEC Recommended Practices can be embedded in coursework to highlight the current research in the field. Students will benefit from learning about the research behind practices that have been shown to be effective.

Parents and families of young children with disabilities can review evidence-based practices and ensure their children are receiving recommended interventions.

Acknowledgments

Thank you to the following individuals and leading experts in the field of early intervention and early childhood special education who contributed to this publication: Betsy Ayankoya, Rashida Banerjee, Tricia Catalino, Camille Catlett, Kevin Dolan, Chelsea Guillen, Kathleen Hebbler, Jeanette McCollum, Mary McLean, Lori E. Meyer, Beth S. Rous, Rosa Milagros Santos, Ilene Schwartz, Patricia Snyder, Jane Squires, Carol M. Trivette, Pam Winton, and Juliann Woods.

A Generation of Recommended Practices

Many of our early childhood special education and early intervention providers entering the field today were not even born or were young children themselves when the DEC Recommended Practices were first developed and published in 1991!

A History of the DEC Recommended Practices

Mary McLean
University of Florida

During the half time of the Kansas-North Carolina NCAA basketball game in 1991, a small group of members from the Division for Early Childhood (DEC) Executive Board met to discuss a process for identifying recommended practices in the field. Although our discussion was interrupted by the second-half of the game and then the great celebration by the Jayhawk fans in the room, a subsequent discussion ensued. The DEC Recommended Practices Task Force was formed. (McLean & Odom, 1996)

The Initial DEC Recommended Practices

AT THE TIME OF THE BEGINNING OF THE RECOMMENDED PRACTICES in 1991, the Division for Early Childhood (DEC), the professional organization for the field of early intervention/early childhood special education, was not yet 20 years old. In 1973, the Board of Governors of the Council for Exceptional Children (CEC), after an initial refusal, approved the establishment of a 10th CEC division, the Division for Early Childhood (DEC). It was the first division to be defined by an age group rather than by a category of disability. The new division moved quickly to establish services for its members and also quickly became politically active. In partnership with CEC, DEC submitted recommendations on bills to create birth to age 5 services under the Education of the Handicapped Act in 1985 and 1986, and in 1986, DEC testified before Congress on S. 2294, the Senate bill precursor to P.L. 99-457, which initiated federal funding for services for all children with disabilities from birth through age 5 (McLean, Sandall, & Smith, in press).

The passage of P.L. 99-457, a celebrated accomplishment, had the effect of greatly increasing the amount of work faced by the young DEC organization. Many states had no services in place, no teacher certification or professional development programs, and no standards for services for the population of young children with disabilities. By 1991, it became clear to the DEC Executive Board that guidance was needed on a national level, and the idea of creating DEC recommendations for practice was born.

The DEC Recommended Practices Task Force, mentioned above, was chaired by Sam Odom and Mary McLean and included eight members from the DEC Executive Committee: Susan Fowler, then president of DEC, Larry Johnson, Mary McEvoy, Susie Perrett, Chris Salisbury, Vicki Stayton, Daphne Thomas, and Barbara Smith, the DEC executive director. The task force developed and carried out plans for identifying what initially was called *best practices*. However, the task force realized that what is determined to be best for one child may not be best for all children. In addition, there was a realization that the practices should change over time as new strategies are proposed and determined through research to be effective. As a result, *recommended practices* was adopted as a more appropriate term.

The task force developed a plan for identifying the initial set of practices. Fourteen strands were identified by the task force and are listed at the end of this article along with the individuals who chaired each strand. The task force decided that a broad base of input would be best for identifying recommended practices within each strand and, as a result, plans were developed to hold workgroups for each strand at the 1991 DEC Conference in St. Louis. Three groups of individuals were asked to come together around each strand at the conference: researchers, practitioners, and families. All DEC members were invited to join a group at the conference. Individual strand chairs invited researchers with a strong knowledge base to participate in their meetings, and the DEC Family Concerns Committee invited families to attend and financially supported their travel to the conference. Input was also possible through mail or phone. Strand groups were asked to consider practices appropriate for children from birth to age 6 with disabilities or delays in development. In addition, six philosophical criteria were identified to guide the work, specifying that the practices should be research-based or values-based, family-centered, multicultural, cross-disciplinary, developmentally and chronologically age appropriate, and normalized.

When the meetings in St. Louis were finished, the practices suggested by each strand group were edited by the corresponding strand chairs and then edited by the task force chairs. A total of 415 practices were identified. The final list of practices was edited into a validation survey that was distributed to 500 people, who were asked whether each practice should become a recommended practice. The criterion was set at 50% for ratings of either *agree* or *strongly agree*. Every practice met this criterion, so all were identified as recommended practices.

Survey participants also were asked how much they thought a practice could be used in settings they are familiar with by rating *frequently, sometimes, rarely,* or *never*. An initial criterion was set at 50% of respondents rating a practice as *frequently*. Eleven of the 14 strands had four or fewer items that met this criterion. A second criterion, which was set at 50% of respondents rating a practice

For three years, this spiral-bound document was the only source for the first version of the DEC Recommended Practices (DEC Task Force on Recommended Practices, 1993).

as either *frequently* or *sometimes*, resulted in most of the practices meeting the criterion (Odom, McLean, Johnson, & LaMontagne, 1995). The difference in the results of using these two criteria have been interpreted as indicating that the field was moving toward implementation of the practices. However, it is important to point out that the initial effort to identify recommended practices for EI/ECSE did not include development of implementation strategies. That work would come later as DEC recognized the importance of implementation strategies for the practices.

The work on the initial DEC Recommended Practices was completed at very little cost. Information about the initial set of recommended practices was contained in two publications (DEC Task Force on Recommended Practices, 1993; Odom & McLean, 1996). The first publication, which was primarily a listing of the practices in each strand, was printed at the local printing shop in Auburn, Alabama, where the author resided. At a time when most people still did not have Internet access, this spiral-bound document was the first and, for three years, the only source for the DEC Recommended Practices. In 1996, the first book about the DEC Recommended Practices was published (Odom & McLean, 1996). This monograph includes articles written by the strand chairs to describe and provide background information on the practices in each strand.

Interestingly, the final paragraph of the introduction to the 1993 document on the DEC Recommended Practices foreshadowed what would become one of the major challenges for the recommended practices effort over time:

> These recommended practices reflect the "state of the art" of EI/ECSE as it exists today. What is "state of the art" today may be archaic five years from now. Only a continuing process of review and revision will maintain the quality of a set of indicators that essentially defines the field. Therefore, with this work we hope that we have begun a process which will involve periodic and continual review and discussion of recommended practice for our field. (DEC Task Force on Recommended Practices, 1993, p. 9)

In 1996, the first book about the DEC Recommended Practices was published (Odom & McLean, 1996).

DEC Recommended Practices Revised

It would be about seven years before the DEC Recommended Practices were revised (Sandall, McLean, & Smith, 2000). As the new century approached, conversations about the initial set of practices included questions about whether the practices were current, whether they reflected the current evidence base, and whether the practices were being used. The data collected in the validation and use study of the initial practices had indicated that they were not widely used in the field (Odom et al., 1995), and it was not clear that use in the field was increasing.

Research in the field was changing, however. In 1997, Michael Guralnick (1997) wrote a book on the effectiveness of early intervention in which he proposed that it was time to stop asking whether early intervention is effective, a question he referred to as "first-generation research." Instead, Guralnick suggested it was time to begin asking what works for which children and under which conditions, questions he referred to as "second-generation research." Guralnick argued that the passage of P.L. 99-457, which mandated services to children with disabilities from birth through age 5, had essentially changed the nature of research that is needed in our field.

Discussions about second-generation research were timely as David Sexton, then vice president of DEC, and Barbara Smith, executive director of DEC, initiated an effort to revise the DEC Recommended Practices. Through a grant proposal to the Office of Special Education Programs of the U.S. Department of Education, funding to revise and update the practices was obtained in 1998. Revision of the recommended practices was focused on two primary goals:

1. To produce an empirically supported set of recommendations for practice with young children with disabilities birth through age 5, their families, and those who work with them.
2. To increase the likelihood of the use and adoption of the recommended practices by identifying "indirect supports" necessary for improving direct service practice, and by formatting and disseminating the practices to increase their use by stakeholder groups such as families, personnel trainers, practitioners, and administrators. (Smith, McLean, Sandall, Snyder, & Ramsey, 2005, pp. 27–28)

Seven years after the initial DEC Recommended Practices were released, a revised set of practices was published (Sandall, McLean, & Smith, 2000).

A "management team" consisting of Barbara Smith, David Sexton, Susan Sandall, and Mary McLean led this work along with strand coordinator Sam Odom; methodology consultants Patricia Snyder, Phil Strain, and Bruce Thompson; and strand chairs as listed at the end of this article. Ten strands were initially identified and were later organized into five direct service strands and two indirect support strands.

Empirical support. A major difference in the development of the second version of the recommended practices was the addition of research evidence for the practices as well as the experiences and values of the field. Focus groups were again held to gather recommendations for practices from stakeholders, including researchers, families, administrators, and practitioners. At the 1998 DEC Conference, initial focus groups were held with those having research expertise in the strand areas. Focus groups with families, practitioners, and administrators were held later in the year. Eventually, the policy/procedures strand was combined with the systems change/leadership strand into the policy, procedures, and systems change strand. The learning environments and cultural/linguistic sensitivity strands were integrated across all strands. The final list of practices included a total of seven strands: five related to direct services and two indirect support strands.

As mentioned above, a major difference between the first set of recommended practices and the second set was the addition of a review of the evidence base during the development of the practices. Initially, the field was asked to recommend professional journals that should be included in the research review. Journals nominated included many from related fields in addition to those in early childhood education and early childhood special education. A total of 48 journals were reviewed for research articles between 1990 and 1998 that met the criteria. The methodology consultants recommended the inclusion of research from randomized controlled trials as well as other methodologies in the effort to identify evidence-based practices (Snyder, Thompson, McLean, & Smith, 2002). Coding sheets were developed for the methodology consultants for group quantitative, single subject, descriptive, qualitative, and mixed method research designs.

A total of 1,018 articles were read and coded by 42 volunteer coders; both a generic and a specialized coding sheet by methodology were completed for each article. Coders were asked to record information about each article and the methodology used and to also identify the recommended practices supported by the research as well as the strand to which the practices should be assigned. To ensure consistency of coding, an additional 29 coders read 33% of the articles and validated the recommended practices identified as well as the strand placement. As a result of the literature review, 835 articles contributed information for the practices. Some articles contributed to more than one practice, leading to a total of 977 recommendations from the literature for practices across the strands.

Once the literature review was completed, the remaining task was to synthesize the practice recommendations from the literature review with the practice recommendations from the researcher focus groups and the stakeholder groups (families, administrators, and practitioners). The result was 250 practices—considerably reduced from the original 415 practices. These 250 practices then were included in the field validation study (McLean, Snyder, Smith, & Sandall, 2002). Like the first set of practices, this field validation asked respondents whether the practice should be a recommended practice (*strongly agree, agree, disagree*, or *strongly disagree*) and the extent to which they see it in practice in programs they are familiar with (*frequently, sometimes, rarely*, and *never*).

Eight hundred individuals representing families, practitioners, higher education personnel, and administrators were asked to respond to the validation questionnaire. All of the practices met the criterion of 50% of the respondents rating each item as *strongly agree* or *agree* for the first question. The most common response to the question about how frequently the practice would be used in programs was *sometimes* for all practices. The second most frequent response was *frequently* for all strands, with the exception of technology and policy/systems change, where *rarely* was the second most frequent response.

Use and adoption of the practices. The first set of DEC Recommended Practices was available only in print. As indicated above, for the first three years, a spiral-bound document was the only print version available. To increase the use and adoption of the second version of the practices, four focus groups were held to determine what formats would be most useful to stakeholders. The stakeholders indicated that they wanted examples of the practices and that they also wanted materials available in different formats: print, video, and Web-based products (Smith et al., 2005). In addition, DEC produced a variety of products to facilitate implementation of the practices: a video demonstrating several of the practices (Division for Early Childhood, 2001), a program assessment (Hemmeter, Joseph, Smith, & Sandall, 2001), and a book devoted to personnel preparation (Stayton, Miller, & Dinnebeil, 2002).

In 2005, a "comprehensive guide for practical application" of the DEC

Five years after publication of the revised recommended practices, a "comprehensive guide for practical application" of the practices was published (Sandall, Hemmeter, Smith, & McLean, 2005).

Recommended Practices was published. Among other things, this guide included examples of the practices as well as lists of resources for each strand that might be useful for implementation (Sandall, Hemmeter, Smith, & McLean, 2005). Also in 2005, DEC published the *DEC Recommended Practices Workbook* (Hemmeter, Smith, Sandall, & Askew, 2005), which facilitated the use of the recommended practices not only by strand but also by activities, such as monitoring child progress and preventing and addressing challenging behavior, by selecting practices from across the strands that support each activity.

In addition to these products, a grant from the Office of Special Education Programs in the U.S. Department of Education awarded to the University of Colorado Denver in partnership with DEC under the leadership of Barbara Smith, then executive director, allowed DEC to study the implementation of the recommended practices in two high-quality programs in Colorado: the Douglas County School District and the Sewall Child Development Center. Focused on the systems developed for implementation of the DEC Recommended Practices in these two sites using the DEC program assessment and action planning forms (Hemmeter, Joseph, et al., 2001), this grant led to documentation of lessons learned in the process and suggestions at the state level for sustaining the change over time (Askew, Smith, Frederick, Heissenbuttel, & Whitman, 2005).

DEC Recommended Practices Timeline

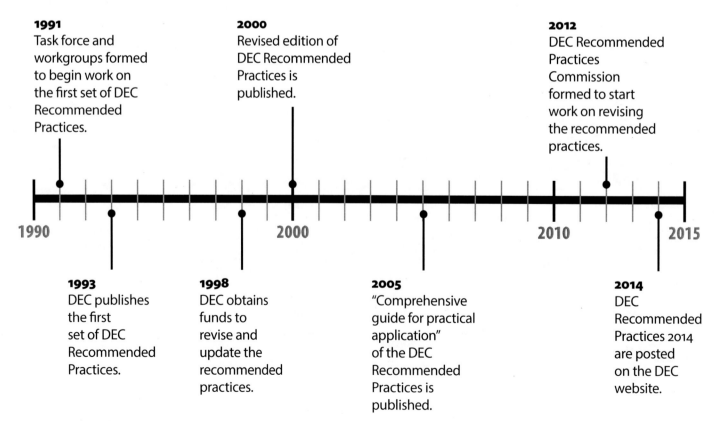

Looking Back

Since that first meeting during halftime of the Kansas-North Carolina basketball game in 1991, hundreds of volunteers filling various roles—practitioners, families, administrators, researchers, and more—have offered their expertise and their time to the development and implementation of the DEC Recommended Practices. As explained in the next article of this monograph by Patricia Snyder and Betsy Ayankoya, work on the recommended practices continued after the second version of the practices. DEC welcomed a third version of the practices in 2014. The vision for the DEC Recommended Practices now includes a process for ongoing review and revision with a clear and continually updated connection to the evidence base. DEC members and others are invited to join DEC in this important work.

References

Askew, L., Smith, B. J., Frederick, L., Heissenbuttel, H., & Whitman, G. (2005). Real life experiences: Tips for using the DEC recommended practices. In S. Sandall, M. L. Hemmeter, B. J. Smith, & M. E. McLean (Eds.), *DEC recommended practices: A comprehensive guide for practical application in early intervention/early childhood special education* (pp. 221–263). Longmont, CO: Sopris West.

DEC Task Force on Recommended Practices. (1993). *DEC recommended practices: Indicators of quality in programs for infants and young children with special needs and their families.* Pittsburgh, PA: Division for Early Childhood.

Division for Early Childhood. (2001). *DEC recommended practices video: Selected strategies for teaching young children with special needs* [Video tape]. Longmont, CO: Sopris West.

Guralnick, M. J. (1997). *The effectiveness of early intervention.* Baltimore, MD: Paul H. Brookes.

Hemmeter, M. L., Joseph, G. E., Smith, B. J., & Sandall, S. (2001). *DEC recommended practices program assessment: Improving practices for young children with special needs and their families.* Longmont, CO: Sopris West.

Hemmeter, M. L., Smith, B. J., Sandall, S., & Askew, L. (2005). *DEC recommended practices workbook: Improving practices for young children with special needs and their families.* Missoula, MT: Division for Early Childhood.

McLean, M. E., & Odom, S. L. (1996). Establishing recommended practices in early intervention/early childhood special education. In S. L. Odom & M. E. McLean (Eds.), *Early intervention/early childhood special education: Recommended practices* (pp. 1–22). Austin, TX: PRO-ED.

McLean, M. E., Sandall, S., & Smith, B. J. (in press). A history of early childhood special education. In B. Reichow, B. A. Boyd, E. E. Barton, & S. L. Odom (Eds.), *Handbook of early childhood special education.* New York, NY: Springer.

McLean, M. E., Snyder, P., Smith, B. J., & Sandall, S. R. (2002). The DEC recommended practices in early intervention/early childhood special education: Social validation. *Journal of Early Intervention, 25,* 120–128. doi:10.1177/105381510202500209

Odom. S. L., & McLean, M. E. (Eds.). (1996). *Early intervention/early childhood special education: Recommended practices.* Austin, TX: PRO-ED.

Odom, S. L., McLean, M. E., Johnson, L. J., & LaMontagne, M. J. (1995). Recommended practices in early childhood special education: Validation and current use. *Journal of Early Intervention, 19,* 1–17. doi:10.1177/105381519501900101

Sandall, S., Hemmeter, M. L., Smith, B. J., & McLean, M. (Eds.). (2005). *DEC recommended practices: A comprehensive guide for practical application in early intervention/early childhood special education.* Longmont, CO: Sopris West.

Sandall, S., McLean, M. E., & Smith, B. J. (2000). *DEC recommended practices in early intervention/early childhood special education.* Longmont, CO: Sopris West.

Smith, B. J., McLean, M. E., Sandall, S., Snyder, P., & Ramsey, A. B. (2005). DEC recommended practices: The procedures and evidence base used to establish them. In S. Sandall, M. L. Hemmeter, B. J. Smith, & M. E. McLean (Eds.), *DEC recommended practices: A comprehensive guide for practical application in early intervention/early childhood special education* (pp. 27–39). Longmont, CO: Sopris West.

Snyder, P., Thompson, B., McLean, M. E., & Smith, B. J. (2002). Examination of quantitative methods used in early intervention research: Linkages with recommended practices. *Journal of Early Intervention, 25,* 137–150. doi:10.1177/105381510202500211

Stayton, V. D., Miller, P. S., & Dinnebeil, L. A. (2002). *DEC personnel preparation in early childhood special education: Implementing the DEC recommended practices.* Longmont, CO: Sopris West.

Strands and Strand Chairs for Original DEC Recommended Practices (1993)

Assessment
John Neisworth

Family Participation
Lisbeth Vincent and Julie Beckett

IFSPs/IEPs
Ann Turnbull and Corrine Garland

Service Delivery Models
Robin McWilliam and Phil Strain

General Curriculum /Intervention Strategies
Mark Wolery

Cognitive Skills Interventions
Carl Dunst

Communication Intervention Strategies
Howard Goldstein

Social/Emotional Intervention Strategies
Mary McEvoy and Paul Yoder

Adaptive Skills Intervention Strategies
Eva Horn

Motor Skills Intervention Strategies
Rebecca Fewell

Transition
Mary Beth Bruder
Lynette Chandler

Personnel Competence
Patricia Miller and Vicki Stayton

Program Evaluation
Scott Snyder

Programs for Gifted Children
Steve Stile

Strands and Strand Chairs for 1998–1999 Focus Groups

Direct Service Strands

Assessment
John Neisworth and Stephen Bagnato

Child-Focused Practices
Mark Wolery

Cultural/Linguistic Sensitivity
Rosa Milagros Santos

Family-based Practices
Carol M. Trivette and Carl Dunst

Interdisciplinary Models
Robin McWilliam

Learning Environments
Mary Beth Bruder

Technology Applications
Kathleen Stremel

Indirect Support Strands

Personnel Preparation
Patricia Miller and Vicki Stayton

Policy/Procedures
Gloria Harbin

Systems Change/Leadership
Chris Salisbury

2

Revising the Division for Early Childhood Recommended Practices: When, Who, and How

PATRICIA SNYDER
University of Florida

BETSY AYANKOYA
University of North Carolina at Chapel Hill

THE DIVISION FOR EARLY CHILDHOOD (DEC) RECOMMENDED PRACtices offer general guidance for practitioners, families, administrators, and other stakeholders about which practices, when implemented as intended, are most likely to be associated with desired outcomes for young children with disabilities or delays, their families, or those working with or on their behalf. The appropriateness or effectiveness of the practices for an individual child and family, however, depends on their characteristics, priorities, and needs; the circumstances under which practices will be used; and the knowledge, skills, and dispositions of those implementing the practices (McLean & Odom, 1996; Snyder, 2006). This is where evidence-based practice comes into play. Evidence-based practice, when the word *practice* is used as a verb, refers to systematic processes used by a family and practitioners to make *individualized* decisions about practice implementation. In evidence-based practice, attention should be focused on child and family characteristics, family values, and in-depth knowledge about a child and family (Buysse, Wesley, Snyder, & Winton, 2006). The recommended practices are useful for helping to guide and inform decisions that result from engaging in evidence-based practice.

Since 2000, practices designated as "recommended" by the Division for Early Childhood (DEC) have been generated by appraising the best-available research evidence, gathering experiential knowledge and wisdom from the field using consensus methods such as focus groups, and conducting field validation activities to verify that identified practices are viewed as important and should be implemented regularly (Smith, McLean, Sandall, Snyder, & Broudy Ramsey, 2005). In addition, five criteria suggested by Peters and Heron (1993) have continued to guide the designation of a practice as recommended: (1) Does the practice have a sound theoretical base? (2) Is the methodological integrity of the research supporting the practice convincing and compelling? (3) Is there consensus about how the practice is defined and implemented within the existing literature? (4) Is there evidence that desired outcomes are consistently produced when the practice is implemented as intended? and (5) Is there evidence of social validity for the practice? Answers to these five questions might change over time as empirical research continues to accumulate or knowledge gained through experiences with implementing recommended practices evolves. Practices might need to be modified or revised as the knowledge base in the field evolves, as views about what constitutes effective practice change, and as new or updated policies that guide practice are disseminated (McLean & Odom, 1996; Snyder, 2006).

In the previous article, McLean describes the history of the DEC recommended practices, beginning with the initial set of practices published in 1993 through the set of practices included in the 2005 volume co-edited by Sandall, Hemmeter, Smith, and McLean. The purpose of this article is to detail the processes used to undertake the revisions to the 2005 recommended practices that resulted in the dissemination of the 2014 DEC Recommended Practices. In addition, we describe the partnership that the Recommended Practices Commission, the Division for Early Childhood, and the Early Childhood Technical Assistance Center (ECTA) have had throughout the revision processes. Finally, we describe how DEC and ECTA continue to work in partnership to support dissemination and implementation of the practices.

Workgroup Appointed to Advise Whether and How to Update Practices

In November 2010, then DEC President Rosa Milagros Santos, with the approval of the DEC Executive Board, convened a workgroup of three members: Judith Carta, Kathleen Hebbeler, and Patricia Snyder. The workgroup received operational support from Sarah Mulligan, a former DEC executive director. The workgroup was asked to meet with representatives from the DEC board and executive director and was charged with the following tasks: (a) gather background information from previous workgroups and individuals involved in the DEC Recommended Practices, (b) propose a plan and scope of work for review by the DEC board for updating the 2005 recommended practices, and (c) ensure the plan included sustainable processes for ongoing review and revision of the recommended practices. The DEC board was particularly interested in a plan that would help ensure the recommended practices would not become static and could be modified or revised, when appropriate. The rationale developed by the workgroup for revising the practices and reviewing and updating the practices on a regular basis was:

> The DEC Recommended Practices are a set of empirically supported recommendations for practice with young children with disabilities birth through age 5, their families, and those who work with them. Given research is ongoing and the contexts in which the practices are enacted are changing, the Recommended Practices need to be

reviewed for possible revision on a regular basis to ensure they reflect current knowledge about effective practices and are relevant and useful for their intended audiences. Also, changes in services delivery, new technologies, and ongoing research on practice implementation underscore the need to reexamine how to disseminate and support utilization of the practices.

Gathering Input From the Field About Recommended Practices

While the workgroup was engaged in its assigned tasks, the DEC Executive Board was simultaneously gathering input from stakeholders about the utility of the recommended practices and issues related to their implementation. Board members also interacted with the workgroup to draft potential taxonomies and frameworks to guide the revision processes. Under the leadership of then President Kristie Pretti-Frontczak, Past President Rosa Milagros Santos, President-Elect Bonnie Keilty, and Vice President Carol M. Trivette, DEC gathered information from previous recommended practices authors and conducted surveys of the DEC membership to gather input from the field. Forums were also held at the annual conference about plans for updating the recommended practices. The results of the information gathering and surveys were shared with the DEC membership through the website and at sessions held at the DEC Conference. In addition, a page on the DEC website provided updated information about what was happening with the recommended practices and to invite participation of the field.

Linking DEC Recommended Practices Revisions and the Early Childhood Technical Assistance Center

In mid-2012, the Office of Special Education Programs released a request for applications (RFA) for the Early Childhood Technical Assistance Center. The RFA included language related to collaborating with DEC to update the 2005 set of recommended practices:

> In year one of the project, collaborate with the DEC to update the current set of DEC recommended practices related to: (1) policies that promote a high-quality, coordinated, and integrated early childhood system and provide a foundation necessary to facilitate the use of recommended practices by providers serving infants, toddlers, and preschool children with disabilities and their families; and (2) effective services and evidence-based interventions that result in positive developmental and learning outcomes for infants, toddlers, and preschool children with disabilities and their families. (U.S. Department of Education, 2012, p. B-11)

Building off the proposed plan and scope of work developed by the workgroup and DEC board as well as input gathered from the field, in mid-2012, DEC prepared a plan of action to revise the recommended practices. This plan was available to any entity responding to the RFA for the ECTA Center. In late 2012, it was announced that the Early Childhood Technical Assistance Center (ECTA) would be awarded to the University of North Carolina at Chapel Hill. Thus, the partnership between DEC and ECTA for updating and revising the recommended practices began.

Plan of Action for Updating and Revising the DEC Recommended Practices

The DEC plan of action included four major components: (1) appoint a national Recommended Practices Commission consisting of 11 to 15 DEC members in good standing who would direct and oversee the revision of the recommended practices; (2) within one year, produce a revised set of DEC Recommend Practices using the initial parameters and framework developed by the workgroup and DEC and endorsed by the field; (3) create multiple platforms to ensure that individuals working with young children with disabilities and their families have access to the practices; and (4) ensure ongoing access to the practices and create a plan to continually update both the practices and the supporting materials and make resources available to professionals and family members.

Under the initial action plan, DEC's Recommended Practices would be revised using a key set of parameters to create a smaller set of recommended practices than the 240 existing practices in the 2005 version. Table 1 shows the parameters specified in the initial plan. The plan described that these parameters and other criteria developed by the Recommended Practices Commission would be systematically applied to the 240 practices to identify a core set of revised practices. The practices would undergo careful review and be fine-tuned by the commission with input from the field. The commission was responsible for verifying that, when implemented as intended, the practices would be expected to inform and improve the quality and outcomes of supports and services provided to young children with disabilities, their families, or the personnel who serve them. Technical advisors would be made available to assist with designing and implementing field validation, empirical literature reviews, and the creation of supporting resources to ensure successful implementation.

> The commission was responsible for verifying that, when implemented as intended, the practices would be expected to inform and improve the quality and outcomes of supports and services.

Appointment of the DEC Recommended Practices Commission

As part of the DEC action plan and consistent with the processes specified in the ECTA grant application, in late 2012 DEC appointed seven initial members of the DEC Recommended Practices Commission: Judith Carta, Kathy Hebbeler, Mary Louise Hemmeter, Mary McLean, Susan Sandall, Barbara Smith, and Patricia Snyder. These individuals had contributed significantly to either the previous recommended practices activities or to setting the parameters and proposing a plan and associated processes for revising the practices. The initial commission members were asked to partner with ECTA to hold an open forum at the 2012 DEC Conference to discuss the proposed changes to the recommended practices and gather stakeholder input. Betsy Ayankoya and Dale Epstein from the Early Childhood Technical Assistance Center were appointed as the ECTA liaisons to the commission, and they worked with the initial members to complete these activities. They actively supported and helped inform the commission's initial and

Table 1
Parameters Contained in Initial Plan to Update DEC Recommended Practices

Parameter	Description
Inform interactions and interventions	DEC Recommended Practices should help inform practitioners' interactions and interventions with young children with disabilities and other special needs and their families.
Build upon and extend foundational practices	DEC Recommended Practices should build upon and extend foundational practices in early childhood education and care, including developmentally appropriate practices for young children (Copple & Bredekamp, 2009).
Include principles and strategies applicable to children, birth to age 5, with disabilities and other special needs and their families	DEC Recommended Practices should highlight those practices specifically known to promote the outcomes of young children who have or are at risk for developmental delays/disabilities and to support their families in accordance with the DEC/NAEYC (2009) position statement on early childhood inclusion.
Reflect universal practices that have applicability across settings, contexts, and groupings	DEC Recommended Practices should be applicable across settings (e.g., classroom, home, community), contexts, and age groups (e.g., birth to 3, 3 to 5).
Based on combination of research-based evidence and knowledge or wisdom gained through experience	DEC Recommended Practices should be based on the best-available research evidence, knowledge, or wisdom gained through implementation experience and field validation.

ongoing work. ECTA created a new page on its website to enable the commission to share its activities and to inform the field about the revision processes.

The initial commission members were charged by DEC with creating a process to review the initial action plan and appointing the remaining commission members following an open call to the field for applications. The call was posted on the DEC website, distributed at the 2012 DEC Conference, and included in DEC publications. The DEC Executive Board set the following guidelines for appointments: (1) no more than 15 members; (2) at least one member who is a parent or family member; (3) at least one individual whose primary role is a practitioner; (4) at least one member representing a related discipline (e.g., speech/language, physical therapy, occupational therapy); and (5) at least one member who is a student enrolled in a personnel preparation program in early intervention/early childhood special education; and (6) all commission members must be DEC members in good standing.

The initial commission members met in December 2012 and selected seven additional commission members from the applicant pool. Appointment letters were sent in January 2013, and six of the seven individuals invited to join the commission accepted: Rashida Banerjee, Tricia Catalino, Chelsea Guillen, Lori E. Meyer, Judy Swett, and Pam Winton. In addition, at the December 2012 meeting, the initial commission members elected a chair, Barbara Smith, and developed a preliminary and updated plan of action and accompanying timelines to guide

Figure 1
Initial Recommended Practices Framework: Practitioner Topic Areas and Other Stakeholders Who Use or Support Implementation

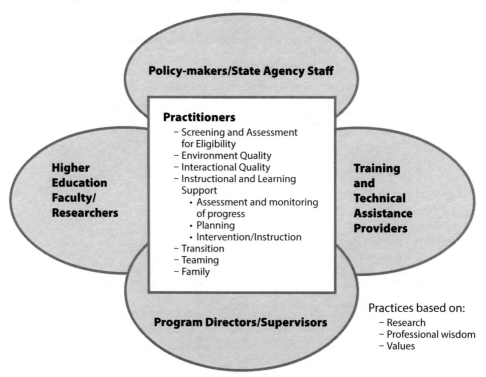

their activities. Once all members were appointed, the commission began its work through conference calls and face-to-face meetings.

Framework, Parameters, Plan of Action, and Timelines for Revision

A framework was developed by the commission to guide the revision process (see Figure 1). As this figure illustrates, based on field input and discussions among commission members, the revised recommended practices would be organized under seven topic areas: assessment, environment, interactional, instructional, transition, teaming, and family. In addition to these seven topic areas, a revised set of leadership practices would be developed.

After the topic areas were identified, the commission developed parameters and definitions for revising the practices under each of the topic areas. Parameters for the practices were described, and key definitions were developed to ensure common understanding of relevant terms. Tables 2 and 3 show examples of key parameters and definitions. In addition to the definitions shown in Table 3, the commission developed working definitions for each of the topic areas. For example, *instructional practices* were defined as intentional and systematic procedures for organizing and structuring children's experiences and observations to maximize learning (Wolery, 2012).

Table 2
Parameters Used to Inform Revisions to the Recommended Practices

Parameter	Description
Population	Young children birth through age 5 who have or are at risk for developmental delays and disabilities. Not limited to those eligible for services under the Individuals with Disabilities Education Act (e.g., children with severe challenging behavior)
High-leverage practices	Practices that are essential to support development and learning of young children birth through age 5, their families, or personnel who work on their behalf and practices most likely to be associated with desired outcomes or impacts when implemented as intended
Sufficient breadth	Number of practices for each topic area is sufficient based on available research, knowledge gained through experience, and values of the field
Observable	Practices should be written so they are observable and clearly describe the actions or behaviors of practitioners
Active voice	Practices should be written in an active voice
Not disability specific	Practices should not be specific to a particular category or type of disability
Build upon and extend foundational practices	Practices should build upon and extend foundational practices in early childhood education and care, including developmentally appropriate practices for young children (DEC/NAEYC, 2009)

Table 3
Key Terms and Definitions Used to Inform Recommended Practices Revisions

Term	Definition
Practice	Approach used to promote development and learning that adults implement within or across contexts when interacting with children, other adults, or materials. To be considered a practice, the approach must be clearly described and commonly understood in the field and literature. Several terms may be used in the literature to refer to the same practice. It is also possible for a named practice to refer to an array of specific procedures or for several practices to be combined as part of a comprehensive approach to promote development and learning (adapted from What Works Clearinghouse, n.d.).
Practitioner	Person who is responsible for and paid to enhance the optimal development of young children who have or are at risk for developmental delays and disabilities. Enhancing the optimal development of young children includes providing care, education, or therapy to the child as well as providing support to the child's family.
Research-based practices	Practices that have been demonstrated to be effective and are supported by evidence in the research literature (Odom et al., 2005). To the extent possible, the evidence base for these practices comes from studies that meet the following criteria: (1) use methodologically sound and high-quality designs (randomized control group, quasi-experimental, and/or single-case experimental design); (2) are reported in the research literature, published in peer-reviewed journals, and replicated by a variety of researchers and research teams; and (3) demonstrate positive effects on specific child or family outcomes.

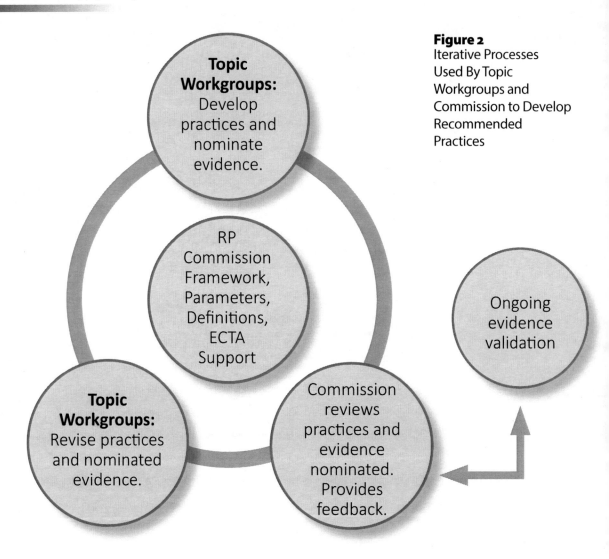

Figure 2
Iterative Processes Used By Topic Workgroups and Commission to Develop Recommended Practices

Given the revision processes had to be completed in about a year, the commission refined its action plan and associated timelines for accomplishing the work. As part of the action plan, the commission decided to identify and recruit individuals with recognized expertise in each of the seven topic areas who would take an active role in the revision processes. These individuals were designated as topic area leaders or co-leaders and were tasked and supported by the commission and ECTA to create topic area workgroups with three to five members. One or two commissioner members served as a liaison to each topic workgroup. The "Participants" section of this book lists the leaders or co-leaders, workgroup members, and the associated commission liaisons.

Each topic workgroup was asked to review the 2005 recommended practices, consider the extant literature related to the topic, and develop a set of 15 or fewer research-based practices using the parameters and definitions developed by the commission. They were asked to provide supporting empirical evidence with accompanying citations for each of the nominated practices. Compiled together, the topic leads submitted the first draft of their proposed practices to the commission in March 2013.

Processes Used to Produce Revised Set of Recommended Practices

After the first draft of revised practices was submitted, several cycles of review by the commission, feedback to the topic workgroups from the commission, and revision by the topic workgroups occurred. Figure 2 illustrates these revision cycles. By December 2013, the revisions had undergone eight review cycles. This version of the practices was distributed for field review via surveys, web-enhanced phone conferences, and listening sessions. In addition, this version was used to conduct further validation of the evidence submitted in support of each of the practices by a group of technical advisors known as the Gap Analysis Group. The processes used to gather stakeholder input at listening sessions, conduct the surveys, and validate the evidence are described in the sections below.

Gathering Stakeholder Input at Listening Sessions

While the various revisions were being made, the commission created opportunities at five national conferences to heighten awareness about the revised practices, to share updates about revision processes, and to gather feedback about the current and revised practices from multiple stakeholders, including researchers, administrators, policy makers, family leaders, family members, and practitioners. These listening sessions enabled the commission to gather information from the field about how the current practices were being used as well as existing barriers to using the practices. Suggestions for revising the practices were solicited. In addition, stakeholders were asked to share ideas about the kind of recommended practices materials and products that would be most useful for them, suggestions about what would enhance their knowledge about and use of the practices, and strategies for helping practitioners and families to implement the practices. Notes from each listening session were reviewed during the commission meetings to inform successive revisions.

Field Surveys About the Draft Practices

The commission decided to conduct field surveys to gather additional input about the revised practices. Version 8, which consisted of 48 practices from the seven topic areas along with the 14 leadership practices, was used to gather this feedback. The ECTA Center planned three web-enhanced phone calls to gather input from the field. The script used to conduct the phone calls is shown in Table 4. Representatives from different stakeholder groups (e.g., state Part C, Section 619, family members, higher education faculty, practitioners, administrators) were invited to participate in the calls.

The overall reaction to the practices was positive. Participants indicated the revised practices were comprehensive, well laid out, and offered a solid foundation for helping to guide practices in the field. Participants commented that the subtopics under Leadership were helpful in understanding key practices. On a call to gather family input, individuals suggested adding a glossary of terms and associated definitions as well as examples of how the practices would look

> The overall reaction to the practices was positive. Participants indicated the revised practices were comprehensive, well laid out, and offered a solid foundation for helping to guide practices in the field.

Table 4
Questions Used to Gather Field Input about DEC Recommended Practices Version 8

Questions

1. What is your overall impression of the scope of the practices presented in this topical area?
    a. What is your reaction to seeing the practices in this topic area?
    b. How well do you think the practices relate to the topic area?
    c. How well do the practices seem to fit in this area?
    d. What do you think about consistency of presentation?
2. Which practices need more clarity or explanation?
    a. Specifically, what is confusing about the wording of the practice?
    b. What word or words might add more clarity to the practice?
    c. What specific question do you have about the particular practice?
3. What practices are missing?
    a. What should be added to the practices in this topic?
    b. Would you provide an example of that practice?
    c. Would you share the reason for making sure this practice is added?
4. Is there anything else you want to share with the commission about the practices in this topic area?
    a. Regarding kinds of products
    b. Formats of products
    c. Ways to implement

when implemented to help family members understand and use the practices. Although information provided from participants was useful, overall participation numbers were low (fewer than 30 participants total across all calls). Because the commission wanted to gather input from a larger number of constituents, it decided to conduct an online survey.

The ECTA Center created the online survey, which was posted on the commission website along with a PDF of Version 8 of the recommended practices. A web link with "voice-over" instructions for completing the survey was distributed through DEC listservs and the ECTA Center newsletter. The survey displayed each practice. Respondents were asked to respond to two questions about each practice using a five-point Likert-type scale ranging from *strongly disagree* (1) to *strongly agree* (5). The questions were: (1) Do you understand the content and intent of the practice as written? and (2) Do you think this practice is important and does it merit being a "recommended practice"? Respondents were provided one space under each practice to enter comments and another space to submit suggested edits to the practice.

Survey participants were not required to respond to the practices listed under all of the topic areas; they could choose the number of topic areas and associated practices to which they wanted to respond. Practices under the Assessment topic area received the most responses ($n = 247$), while practices under the Interaction topic area received the fewest responses ($n = 132$). Across all topic areas and practices, there were 1,439 responses submitted. More than 50% of respondents were current DEC members, and more than 20% were families that had a member with a disability or delay. Results showed that, on average, respondents understood the content and intent of the practices as written (means ranged from 4.3 to 4.75). Respondents thought most of the practices were important and merited being a recommended practice (means ranged from 4.25 to 4.78). Responses to the open-ended sections of the survey were summarized and themes were identified.

To gather additional field input, the commission created targeted opportunities for participants at two conferences to review the draft practices and participate in group discussions about the practices, their utility, and resources that would be useful to support their implementation. Consistent with the online survey, information was also gathered about the content and intent of each practice and whether the practice warranted inclusion in the revised practices.

At the first conference, more than 30 administrators at the 2013 national Improving Data, Improving Outcomes conference reviewed and provided suggestions for the Leadership practices. They outlined the necessary supports and structures that would enable practitioners to implement practices. Participants suggested revised wording for several of the Leadership practices and recommended a glossary of terms and accompanying definitions be developed.

At the second conference, approximately 20 participants in two "early-bird" sessions at the 2013 DEC Conference reviewed the practices from the seven practitioner-focused topic areas. Participants discussed the topic areas in small groups facilitated by commission members and ECTA. They provided feedback about wording changes for some practices, recommended revised sequencing, and suggested combining several practices to reduce redundancy. The participants also suggested that implementation of the practices would be enhanced with supports, resources, and materials, including examples, glossaries, and videos showing how the practices could be implemented.

Summaries from the phone calls, results from the online survey, and information gathered at the conferences were shared with the commission. These data, along with information from the evidence validation activities, were used to revise the recommended practices and to produce the final version (Division for Early Childhood, 2014).

Evidence Validation Activities

Given the accelerated timelines for producing a revised set of recommended practices in one year, the commission determined it would not be feasible to conduct comprehensive literature reviews to gather information about the status of the best-available evidence. Instead, processes for validating the evidence nominated by the topic workgroups and for aligning relevant studies from the database of the empirical literature used to inform the 2000 and 2005 recommended practices were developed and approved by the commission, ECTA, and the DEC Executive Board. The evidence validation processes were overseen by a group of technical advisors from the commission, ECTA, the DEC research community, and the DEC board known as the Gap Analysis Group. The "Participants" section of this book lists members of this group. A three-step evidence validation process was used.

The first step involved aligning relevant studies from the empirical research literature database used when the 2000 and 2005 versions of the recommended

> Participants suggested that implementation of the practices would be enhanced with supports, resources, and materials, including examples, glossaries, and videos showing how the practices could be implemented.

practices were developed. Two technical advisors from the Gap Analysis Group obtained the database and aligned relevant studies from this database with the revised recommended practices. A "crosswalk" document was created. This document showed how the study aligned with a previous recommended practice and its proposed alignment with a revised practice. Five other technical advisors reviewed the proposed alignment between the empirical study and the revised recommended practice. They agreed or disagreed that a study aligned with a revised practice. Percent of agreement was calculated and exceeded an 80% standard.

The second step was to validate evidence nominated by the topic workgroups in support of each revised practice. The purpose was to determine whether studies cited as evidence for a practice demonstrated reliable associations between implementation of the practice (or aspects of the practice) and discernable outcomes or benefits for children, families, or practitioners. In addition, the type of evidence (e.g., experimental, quasi-experimental, single-case design) that supports each recommended practice (Dunst, in press) was categorized. Using systematic processes and a coding framework developed by Dunst, nominated evidence was reviewed. Evidence "gaps" were identified to guide future systematic evidence reviews and to help advance research agendas in the field.

The third step, which is ongoing, is to develop, pilot, and disseminate systematic and ongoing processes that can be used by the field to appraise the best-available research evidence in support of the revised practices and to inform the conduct of summative, systematic, and meta-analytic reviews of the empirical literature related to each of the recommended practices. This work will further build the evidence base for the revised recommended practices and indicate for the commission and the field when practices might need to be modified or new practices developed.

Support Dissemination and Implementation in Collaboration With ECTA and Others

As noted previously, the revised recommended practices were disseminated to the field in June 2014. A glossary of terms and accompanying definitions and examples have been developed by the commission and are scheduled for distribution in early 2015. The evidence validation work in support of the recommended practices is ongoing.

The ECTA Center has been particularly interested in highlighting the recommended practices as they were revised and developing ways to support their use to improve outcomes for young children and their families. For example, the ECTA Center created and invited individuals to participate in a Family Collaborative Partner Group, which consists of representatives from family organizations and family members of children with disabilities in state leadership roles (e.g., members of state Interagency Coordinating Councils [ICCs], advocacy groups). The first activity the group was invited to participate in was a meeting in conjunction with the IDEA Leadership Conference. The group discussed the development of the recommended practices and how the ECTA Center could make these practices more relevant to the field and particularly for families of young children with disabilities. The members have continued to share the critical perspectives about how to make the practices more accessible to families and the types of products (e.g., written materials, training packages, videos) that are needed to help families support their children's development and learning.

To address issues of implementation and sustainability of the DEC Recommended Practices, the ECTA Center provides intensive training and technical assistance (TA) to a limited number of states on implementing, scaling up, and sustaining evidence-based approaches for improving outcomes for young children through RP²: Reaching Potentials through Recommended Practices. This effort focuses on the practices that are most likely to increase child engagement. All tools, processes, and materials that are developed through the intensive TA efforts are available for use by all states. In addition to tools developed for intensive work, the ECTA Center is engaged in developing complementary materials, including practice guides and self-assessment instruments, to support widespread use of the recommended practices.

Through systematic planning, collaborations between DEC and ECTA, and substantial efforts of the DEC Executive Board, DEC Executive Office, and the membership, including the topic workgroups, the commission, and the Gap Analysis Group, the recommended practices have been revised. Moreover, processes have been put into place to ensure reviews and updates occur on a regular basis. The revised set of practices has been made widely available and support for their implementation is ongoing.

References

Buysse, V., Wesley, P. W., Snyder, P., & Winton, P. (2006). Evidence-based practice: What does it really mean for the early childhood field? *Young Exceptional Children, 9*(4), 2–11. doi:10.1177/109625060600900401

Copple, C., & Bredekamp, S. (2009). *Developmentally appropriate practices in early childhood programs serving children from birth through age 8*. Washington, DC: National Association for the Education of Young Children.

DEC/NAEYC. (2009). *Early childhood inclusion: A joint position statement of the Division for Early Childhood (DEC) and the National Association for the Education of Young Children (NAEYC)*. Chapel Hill: The University of North Carolina, FPG Child Development Institute.

Division for Early Childhood. (2014). *DEC recommended practices in early intervention/early childhood special education 2014*. Retrieved from http://www.dec-sped.org/recommendedpractices

Dunst, C. J. (in press). Role of research syntheses for identifying evidence-based early childhood intervention practices. In B. Reichow, B. A. Boyd, E. E. Barton, & S. L. Odom (Eds.), *Handbook of early childhood special education*. New York, NY: Springer.

McLean, M. E., & Odom. S. L. (1996). Establishing recommended practices in early intervention/early childhood special education. In S. L. Odom & M. E. McLean (Eds.), *Early intervention/early childhood special education: Recommended practices* (pp. 1–22). Austin, TX: PRO-ED.

Odom, S. L., Brantlinger, E., Gersten, R., Horner, R. H., Thompson, B., & Harris, K. (2005). Research in special education: Scientific methods and evidence-based practices. *Exceptional Children, 71*, 137–148.

Peters, M. T., & Heron, T. E. (1993). When the best is not good enough: An examination of best practice. *Journal of Special Education, 26*, 371–385. doi:10.1177/002246699302600403

Sandall, S., Hemmeter, M. L., Smith, B. J., & McLean, M. E. (Eds). (2005). *DEC recommended practices: A comprehensive guide for practical application in early intervention/early childhood special education.* Longmont, CO: Sopris West.

Smith, B. J., McLean, M. E., Sandall, S., Snyder, P., & Broudy Ramsey, A. (2005). DEC recommended practices: The procedures and evidence base used to establish them. In S. Sandall, M. L. Hemmeter, B. J. Smith, & M. E. McLean (Eds.), *DEC recommended practices: A comprehensive guide for practical application in early intervention/early childhood special education* (pp. 27–39). Longmont, CO: Sopris West.

Snyder, P. (2006). Best-available research evidence. In V. Buysse & P. W. Wesley (Eds.), *Evidence-based practice in the early childhood field* (pp. 35–70). Washington, DC: Zero to Three.

U.S. Department of Education. (2012). *Application for new grants under the Individuals With Disabilities Education Act (IDEA): Technical assistance and dissemination to improve services and results for children with disabilities — Early Childhood Technical Assistance Center* (CFDA 84.326P). Washington, DC: Author.

What Works Clearinghouse. (n.d.). WWC evidence review protocol for early childhood education for children with disabilities (Version 2.0). Washington, DC: Author.

Wolery, M. (2012). Voices from the field. *Young Exceptional Children, 15*(4), 41–44. doi:10.1177/1096250612466379

3

LEADERSHIP

Setting the Course and Steering the Ship

KATHLEEN HEBBELER
SRI International

Anyone who has ever worked for a really terrific boss has experienced firsthand how good leadership makes a difference. What was it about that person that made him or her so good? Chances are the person made sure things ran smoothly. This boss might have been pleasant and easy to interact with but probably had a lot of other positive characteristics as well. This good boss made staff feel supported, maybe even inspired them to do a better job. This boss also probably understood what staff needed to do their jobs well and worked to make sure they had what they needed.

The Leadership recommended practices speak to the importance of providing all practitioners with those ever-so-important good bosses. As the introduction to the Leadership recommended practices notes and as the DEC position statement on leadership affirms, everyone can be a leader, including practitioners, family members, students, higher education faculty, advocates, and others (Division for Early Childhood, 2014, 2015). The Leadership recommended practices, however, apply to a specific category of leader, "those in positions of leadership or authority in providing services to all young children who have or are at risk for developmental delays/disabilities and their families" (Division for Early Childhood, 2014, pg. 4). These individuals include state, regional, and local program directors and administrators; early childhood coordinators; building principals; and assistant directors and coordinators. To distinguish these leaders in positions of authority from others who also serve as leaders in early intervention (EI) and early childhood special education (ECSE), the term *administrative leaders* will be used to describe those individuals who are the focus of the Leadership recommended practices.

As is apparent from the list above, there are many different types of administrative leaders in EI/ECSE. The variety of leaders is directly related to the diversity of the delivery systems across states and even across localities within states. Those providing services work in a variety of different public and private organizations and, therefore, for a variety of different types of administrative leaders. Practitioners in public school buildings will see and feel the influence of a building principal who may be a visionary with a strong commitment to young children—or have limited knowledge of early childhood and special education. A small private early intervention program could have a director who is a former practitioner and is intimately familiar with the day-to-day experiences of providers.

Alternately, EI services could be provided in a large organization with a much broader mission and a director with little knowledge of EI. State EI/ECSE administrative leaders could have worked as providers or local administrators before joining state government, or they might have come to their current position from another division or state agency and have little working knowledge of the program.

Regardless of the leaders' background or knowledge of EI/ECSE, these individuals in positions of authority play a critical role in ensuring that all young children with disabilities and their families receive high-quality supports and services. How these individuals carry out their day-to-day responsibilities matters a great deal because they influence or even create the conditions that allow those working directly with children and families to implement the other seven areas of the DEC Recommended Practices.

Leaders, Practitioners, and the EI/ECSE System

Appreciating the critical role that effective administrative leaders play in the provision of high-quality services and good outcomes for children and families requires understanding the nature of the system that makes EI/ECSE service delivery possible. The heart of early intervention and early childhood special education is the interaction between the practitioner and the child and the child's family (Hebbeler, Spiker, & Kahn, 2012). These interactions are the focus of most of the DEC Recommended Practices. What is not obvious to families, and to many practitioners as well, is the system in which these practices are embedded. Why is it that an early intervention program exists in a community? Why is it that assessment in one county looks different from assessment in another? Why is it that a preschool child with a developmental delay is attending the state's PreK program rather than a special school? What had to happen so that the early childhood special education teacher could work with the PreK teacher to find ways to embed instruction within and across routines for the child with a delay? The answer to these questions requires understanding the multiple components that make up the system in which EI/ECSE services are delivered and the contribution that administrative leaders make to how well or poorly the system operates.

One important element in the EI/ECSE system is the legal foundation for the provision of services. The delivery of early intervention and early childhood special education is governed by both federal (IDEA, the Individuals with Disabilities

> Regardless of the leaders' background or knowledge of EI/ECSE, these individuals in positions of authority play a critical role in ensuring that all young children with disabilities and families receive high-quality supports and services.

Education Act) and state laws. The federal law stipulates, most importantly, that ECSE services must be provided to all children who are eligible (Individuals with Disabilities Education Act, 2004). The same applies to EI services if the state chooses to participate in the program. The federal law requires that the state agency ensure that all local entities in the state are providing services according to IDEA's provisions. Thus, some of the responsibilities of state administrative leaders come directly from IDEA.

When an earlier version of IDEA was amended in 1986 to create what today is nationwide access to EI and ECSE services, this significant amendment necessitated building an infrastructure to deliver those services. *Infrastructure* means roads, bridges, electric wires, cell phone towers, and water pipes when used to refer to basic services in cities and towns. For EI/ECSE, *infrastructure* refers to the programs that deliver services as well as the system that allows, supports, and ensures that local programs are providing high-quality services consistent with the provision of state and federal laws.

Components of the EI/ECSE infrastructure include the institutions of higher education that train the personnel providing EI/ECSE; the state agencies that both support and monitor local service delivery; the policies and procedures created by these agencies that determine among other things how services will be funded and stipulate what can and cannot be paid for; and the personnel standards that lay out the requirements for being an EI/ECSE provider. A framework developed for states to examine and improve their EI/ECSE system identifies six components of a state system: governance, finance, personnel/workforce, quality standards, accountability and quality improvement, and the data system (Early Childhood Technical Assistance Center, 2015).

And where are EI/ECSE's administrative leaders in this system? Quite simply, everywhere. The EI/ECSE system is not a faceless machine running on autopilot. The system is guided by those individuals at the state level who are developing the policies and procedures, making the funding decisions, creating professional development opportunities, advocating for more funding, setting a vision for service delivery around the state, submitting the paperwork to get next year's funding from the federal government, and generally carrying out the responsibilities that the law requires of the state agency. Much closer to children and families, local program leaders are managing staff and budgets, advocating for more funding, building staff competencies, submitting required paperwork (everyone does paperwork), working with colleagues in other agencies, using data to check program performance, and making needed adjustments to bring the program more in line with its mission and vision for delivering high-quality services and supports. At least, that is what we are hoping they are doing. The Leadership recommended practices were developed to articulate the key responsibilities of administrative leaders at both the local and state level in building and enhancing the EI/ECSE system.

Before turning to the content of the practices themselves, it is important to underscore a critical feature of any system: Everything is interrelated. As noted in the introduction to the Leadership recommend practices, administrative leaders have authority and responsibility. What they don't have is control. They likely have decision-making authority over how some portion of their budget is spent; they may have little influence over the total amount of that budget. A leader with an inspiring vision of what service delivery should look like and with data to identify gaps and solutions might work in an agency that is not receptive to change.

An individual's ability to fully implement the Leadership recommended practices will be constrained or enhanced by the unique characteristics of the agency or organization in which he or she works. Other external factors such as the availability of personnel or training opportunities within the state can be facilitators or significant barriers to quality services. The Leadership recommended practices are not meant to imply that administrative leaders can work miracles, but there is an expectation that good leaders identify when and where change is needed and serve as the champions to try to bring it about.

The Content of the Practices

The Leadership recommended practices address the multiple and varied responsibilities of an EI/ECSE administrative leader. As discussed in the DEC position statement on leadership, there is an important distinction between managers and leaders that is sometimes overlooked in early childhood (Division for Early Childhood, 2015; Goffin & Rous, 2015). Managing refers to the day-to-day operations of programs encompassing responsibilities such as planning, policies and procedures, budgets, and supervising personnel.

Leadership, on the other hand, has to do with planning and organizing around a shared vision, adapting to changing circumstances, and setting direction. Leadership means working to influence others to act in ways consistent with values, aspirations, and expectations (Kagan, 2013). The Leadership recommended practices address both the managerial and leadership aspects of administrative leadership.

Visionary Management

Most of the Leadership recommended practices speak to functions internal to the program and over which an administrative leader could be expected to have some control. Even with these recommended practices, any individual leader might be somewhat constrained in his or her capacity to implement a practice because of limited authority or limited resources. The distinction between management and leadership notwithstanding, the recommended practices that address internal program operations also reflect vision, values, and the importance of inspiring others. They require individuals to understand and embrace the vision and values of EI/ECSE, which are reflected in all the DEC Recommended Practices. For example:

- Leaders create a culture and a climate in which practitioners feel a sense of belonging and want to support the organization's mission and goals.
- Leaders develop and implement policies, structures, and practices that promote shared decision making with practitioners and families.
- Leaders develop and implement an evidence-based professional development system or approach that provides practitioners a variety of supports to ensure they have the knowledge and skills needed to implement the DEC Recommended Practices.

Note the values embodied in these practices: the importance of a sense of belonging, of shared decision making, of professional development in general, and of approaches that are based on evidence in particular. The message conveyed in these and other practices is that a good leader works to ensure that day-to-day program operations reflect these and other values that are essential for high-quality EI/ECSE services.

Several practices speak to leaders creating the conditions so practitioners can implement the DEC Recommended Practices. These "conditions" cover the gamut of what needs to be in place for practitioners to do a good job. They include ensuring staff have the knowledge to implement the Recommended Practices. They also include making sure that practitioners have the time and scheduling flexibility needed to work together as a team with the family and have access to adequate and appropriate materials, including technology and other resources. Implementation science has identified various "drivers" that influence successful implementation of practices. An especially relevant driver for the Leadership recommended practices is facilitative administration, which refers to administrators who facilitate organizational change, monitor implementation, and ensure improvement in critical areas such as staff competence (Bertram, Blase, & Fixsen, 2013; Metz, Halle, Bartley, & Blasberg, 2013). The effective leader structures the program environment to reflect the values of EI/ECSE and to facilitate practitioner implementation of the recommended practices.

Much like we are not especially aware of the contributions that any individual organ in the body makes to our overall health until something goes wrong, the "conditions" practitioners need to implement the recommended practices are sometimes only obvious in their absence. Negative examples include

> Leadership has to do with planning and organizing around a shared vision, adapting to changing circumstances, and setting direction.

reimbursement policies that restrict service delivery in some way or schedules that do not support professionals and the family coming together as a team. Practitioners may be stifled in their ability to do the right thing by "ghost" policies—policies that are not real, but people behave as if they are. Good leaders work to create policies and procedures that support the recommended practices and expose ghost policies that are standing in the way of their implementation. Good leaders set tone, expectations, and a vision for the implementation of the recommended practices.

Unfortunately, our field has far too many stories of administrators who rather than creating these conditions are themselves the barriers to recommended practices. There are stories of the early childhood special and general education teachers who can't teach the way they know they should because they have a building administrator who does not understand the recommended practices or even developmentally appropriate practice (Copple & Bredekamp, 2009). Or early interventionists who work in large agencies with supervisors who do not understand the key principles, such as family preference or building on family strength and capacity, that are embodied in the recommended practices. The Leadership recommended practices apply to all of the individuals who are in positions of authority over EI/ECSE service delivery, including those who do not have a background in the field. We hope practitioners and professional organizations will share the recommended practices with administrative leaders who might not otherwise have the opportunity to learn about them. The diversity of the EI/ECSE service delivery system and overall early care and education system means that services are overseen by many kinds of leaders. The goal is to have all of them working to create the conditions for high-quality services and supports.

Collaboration and Advocacy

Some of the Leadership recommended practices are more externally focused, speaking to the need for leaders to work across programs and agencies and to advocate for change. The practices address several kinds of collaboration. One is across agencies and other systems to create coordinated and inclusive systems of services and supports. The EI/ECSE service delivery systems are only one component of the larger general early care and education (ECE) system. Although many states are moving to build more unified or coordinated approaches to early care and education, there is still much work to be done (Kagan & Kauerz, 2012). Until the multiple programs that make up ECE, such as child care, Early Head Start, Head Start, state PreK, and of course, EI and ECSE, are woven into a more unified system, EI/ECSE leaders will need to reach out to their counterparts in other programs and agencies so young children with disabilities are welcomed and served appropriately in all programs in their communities. EI/ECSE leaders need to build the bridges that connect the specialists they oversee with the ECE providers in other programs because it is those bridges that allow young children with disabilities to be fully included in those programs.

The DEC/NAEYC position statement on inclusion lists the defining features of inclusion as access, participation, and supports (Division for Early Childhood & National Association for the Education of Young Children, 2009).

> EI/ECSE leaders need to build the bridges that connect the specialists they oversee with the ECE providers in other programs because it is those bridges that allow young children with disabilities to be fully included in those programs.

EI/ECSE leaders can contribute the expertise needed to help make programs accessible. Supported by leadership, EI/ECSE practitioners can work with general early care and education providers so the young children with disabilities have the necessary accommodations and supports to fully participate in these programs. Finally, EI/ESCE leaders need to work with their other ECE counterparts to build an infrastructure that supports inclusion. That infrastructure would include the mechanisms for delivering the professional development to implement the recommended practices in inclusive settings, the communication mechanisms needed to share information across programs, and the policies that address issues such as funding for general and special education staff to work collaboratively and staffing ratios that ensure adequate support for children with disabilities. Building this infrastructure is a tall order, and EI/ECSE leaders at the local and state level are uniquely positioned to play a major role in making it happen.

Another kind of collaboration addressed in the recommended practices speaks to the need for EI/ECSE administrative leaders to work with other agencies and programs to implement ongoing screening. Identifying children who need services and getting these children into services as early as possible remains an ongoing challenge (Kavanagh, Gerdes, Sell, Jimenez, & Guevara, 2012). Pediatricians and child care providers can be important referral sources if an effective infrastructure is in place for screening and referral (American Academy of Pediatrics Committee on Children with Disabilities, 2001; National Infant and Toddler Child Care Initiative, 2010).

The administrative leaders of EI/ESCE programs at the local and state level are well positioned to make a major contribution to the building of such an infrastructure.

One last and critically important area of collaboration for administrative leaders at the state and local level is collaboration around the development of state competencies that align with DEC, Council for Exceptional Children (CEC), and other national professional standards. The establishment of appropriate professional standards for those delivering EI/ECSE services continues to be a problem for the field (Bruder & Dunst, 2005; Hebbeler, Spiker, & Kahn, 2012). The DEC Recommended Practices are not a substitute for having highly trained professionals in the EI/ECSE workforce. As stated clearly in the introduction to the practices, it is assumed that those implementing the practices have foundational knowledge and engage in ongoing professional development (Division for Early Childhood, 2014, p. 3). By collaborating to put appropriate professional standards in place, EI/ECSE administrative leaders are working to ensure that all practitioners will be able to implement the practices early in their careers and that all children and families receive uniformly high-quality services. The practices also call explicitly for advocacy, directing leaders to work across levels and sectors to advocate for policies and resources. Adequate funding for EI/ECSE has always been problematic (Bruder, 2010). Significant recent reduction in federal funding for EI resulted in some states narrowing their early intervention eligibility criteria and instituting family fees (Hebbeler, Greer, & Hutton, 2011). The federal per child contributions for ECSE has declined from $803 in 1992 to $471 in 2013 (Lazara, Danaher, & Goode, 2014). EI/ECSE leaders cannot solve the funding problem alone, but they can play a major role in informing policy-makers of the importance of services for young children with disabilities and the need to fund those services adequately.

Taking Care of Your Professional Self

Finally, two Leadership recommended practices are "personal practices" in that they address how administrative leaders need to be active professionals in the field by belonging to professional organizations and staying current in the field. Leaders also are expected to model the principles embodied in the DEC Code of Ethics, positions statements, and the recommended practices. On the personal front, there isn't a recommended practice that tells leaders to eat right, exercise, and get plenty of sleep, but maybe there should be because being a good leader in EI/ECSE definitely requires being at the top of one's game.

The Leadership Practices and the Previous Recommended Practices

Those familiar with the previous DEC Recommended Practices (Sandall, McLean, & Smith, 2000) might be wondering what happened to the indirect support practices. The previous practices were divided into "direct services" and "indirect supports." The indirect supports, the fundamentals necessary for high-quality direct services to occur, addressed policies, procedures, and systems change along with personnel preparation. These practices covered a variety of topics, such as what policies should contain, what administrators should do, and what families and professionals should do to shape policies. The sentences for these practices started with a variety of subjects such as "public policies," "administrators," "leadership and systems change," and "resources." This kind of variation in sentence structure also occurred in the direct practices; both sets described what was expected to happen but not always who was expected to do it.

In revising the practices, the Recommended Practices Commission decided that each of the new direct practices would start with the word *practitioners* to clarify who is expected to implement each practice. Because DEC is a membership organization, the commission wanted the revised practices to specify which category of members would be expected to carry out the new practices, including the former practices that addressed policies, procedures, and systems change. In revising these practices, the commission chose to identify leaders as doers, and thus the new Leadership recommended practices were created. There is not a one-to-one correspondence or mapping of the old practices to the new Leadership recommended practices, but the initial kernels for the Leadership recommended practices were drawn from concepts contained in the former support practices. In the process of revising the recommended practices to be written for the administrative leader, the commission also identified a number of important practices for leaders that were not addressed in the previous set of practices.

Implementation of the Leadership Recommended Practices

The provision of high-quality EI/ECSE services and the ability of children and families to experience good outcomes depend on the actions of the professionals who work in EI/ECSE. The DEC Recommended Practices were developed to provide clear guidance as to what those actions should entail. Those who oversee EI/ECSE programs at the state and local level play a unique and essential role in the EI/ECSE system. They hold the vision for EI/ECSE. They promote it in their programs through policies, procedures, and other actions that establish conditions that reflect the values and principles embodied in the recommended practices. They promote it in their communities and agencies by informing others of the importance of EI/ECSE services and the need to set policies, including adequate funding, that will allow the vision to stay or become reality. These leaders sometimes practice their craft behind the scenes, but they are key players in the system nevertheless. The Leadership recommended practices stand both as a guide for EI/ECSE leaders and an acknowledgement of the importance of their contributions.

> Those who oversee EI/ECSE programs at the state and local level play a unique and essential role in the EI/ECSE system. They hold the vision for EI/ECSE.

References

American Academy of Pediatrics Committee on Children with Disabilities. (2001). Developmental surveillance and screening of infants and young children. *Pediatrics, 108*, 192–196. doi:10.1542/peds.108.1.192

Bertram, R. M., Blase, K. A., & Fixsen, D. L. (2013, April). *Improving programs and outcomes: Implementation frameworks 2013*. Paper presented at the Bridging the Research and Practice Gap Symposium, Houston, TX.

Bruder, M. B. (2010). Early childhood intervention: A promise to children and families for their future. *Exceptional Children, 76*, 339–355. doi:10.1177/001440291007600306

Bruder, M. B., & Dunst, C. J. (2005). Personnel preparation in recommended early intervention practices: Degree of emphasis across disciplines. *Topics in Early Childhood Special Education, 25,* 25–33. doi:10.1177/02711214050250010301

Copple, C., & Bredekamp, S. (Eds.). (2009). *Developmentally appropriate practice in early childhood programs: Serving children from birth through age 8* (3rd ed.). Washington, DC: National Association for the Education of Young Children.

Division for Early Childhood. (2014). *DEC recommended practices in early intervention/early childhood special education 2014.* Retrieved from http://www.dec-sped.org/recommendedpractices

Division for Early Childhood. (2015). *DEC position statement: Leadership in early intervention and early childhood special education.* Retrieved from http://www.dec-sped.org/papers

Division for Early Childhood, & National Association for the Education of Young Children. (2009). *Early childhood inclusion: A joint position statement of the Division for Early Childhood (DEC) and the National Association for the Education of Young Children (NAEYC).* Retrieved from http://www.dec-sped.org/papers

Early Childhood Technical Assistance Center. (2015, January). *A system framework for building high-quality early intervention and preschool special education programs.* Chapel Hill, NC: Author. Retrieved from http://ecta-center.org/~pdfs/pubs/ecta-system_framework.pdf

Goffin, S. G., & Rous, B. (2015). Revisting early childhood education's governance choices. In S. L. Kagan & R. E. Gomez (Eds.), *Early childhood goverance: Choices and consequences* (pp. 165–175). New York, NY: Teachers College Press.

Hebbeler, K., Greer, M., & Hutton, B. (2011). From then to now: The evolution of Part C. *Zero To Three, 31*(4), 4–10.

Hebbeler, K., Spiker, D., & Kahn, L. (2012). Individuals with Disabilities Education Act's early childhood programs: Powerful vision and pesky details. *Topics in Early Childhood Special Education, 31,* 199–207. doi:10.1177/0271121411429077

Individuals with Disabilities Education Act, 20 U.S.C. § 1400 (2004).

Kagan, S. L. (2013, December). *Leadership for young children.* Paper presented at the Early Childhood Personnel Center Leadership Institute, Hartford, CT. Retrieved from http://www.ecpcta.org/pdfs/Leadership_FINAL_12-9-13.pdf

Kagan, S. L., & Kauerz, K. (Eds.). (2012). *Early childhood systems: Transforming early learning.* New York, NY: Teacher College Press.

Kavanagh, J., Gerdes, M., Sell, K., Jimenez, M., & Guevara, J. (2012, Summer). *SERIES: An integrated approach to supporting child development.* Philadelphia, PA: PolicyLab. Retrieved from http://policylab.chop.edu/evidence-action-brief/series-integrated-approach-supporting-child-development-0

Lazara, A., Danaher, J., & Goode, S. (2014). *Section 619 preschool program: Federal appropriations and national child count 1977–2013.* Chapel Hill, NC: Early

Childhood Technical Assistance Center. Retrieved from http://ectacenter.org/~pdfs/growthcomp.pdf

Metz, A., Halle, T., Bartley, L., & Blasberg, A. (2013). The key components of successful implementation. In T. Halle, A. Metz, & I. Martinez-Beck (Eds.), *Applying implementation in early childhood programs and systems* (pp. 21–42). Baltimore, MD: Paul H. Brookes.

National Infant and Toddler Child Care Initiative. (2010). *Infant/toddler development, screening, and assessment*. Washington, DC: Author.

Sandall, S., McLean, M. E., & Smith, B. J. (2000). *DEC recommended practices in early intervention/early childhood special education*. Longmont, CO: Sopris West.

4

ASSESSMENT

Guiding Principles for Accurate and Efficient Decision Making

JANE SQUIRES
University of Oregon

ASSESSMENT INCLUDES A VARIETY OF METHODS USED TO EVALUATE, measure, and document skills. From appraising the intellectual capacity of adults to identifying school-age children in need of extra help, assessment has long been around to help us make appraisals of human behavior. Assessment, in the context of this monograph, can be defined as a process for gathering information to make decisions about the teaching and learning of young children.

Assessment for young children with disabilities is embedded within our federal and state laws related to the Individuals With Disabilities Education Act (2004), a federal law that regulates services for children with disabilities from birth to age 21. IDEA provides clear requirements for using assessments to establish children's eligibility for early intervention/early childhood special education (EI/ECSE) services as well educational planning (i.e., individualized family service plans or individualized education programs). Child Find and screening processes also call for using standardized norm-referenced tests to identify children who may need specialized IDEA services.

To meet IDEA regulations as well as to provide children with optimal learning experiences, we "assess" so that we can make important decisions accurately and efficiently: Is Dorian eligible for these services? Is Drake learning skills important for independence at home? Will Avril learn faster through guided play or direct instruction? What events are difficult for Jenny? How can I improve her rate of learning new skills?

In the ideal world, assessment allows us to put on glasses or "lenses" with which to see children's skills in a new way, perhaps with more outline or definition. Assessment should provide an objective lens through which to view children's behavior to make decisions that assist in planning optimal learning activities. Assessment should add to what we know about children and help us figure out the best ways to increase their developmental repertoire and enhance their social-emotional competence. Ideally, we use assessment results to maximize learning opportunities and provide appropriate support and resources to the child and family.

To those of us in the early childhood world, assessment often brings as many challenges as benefits. In attempting to capture—through measurement and documentation—what a child can do and how she does it, practitioners are often faced with a dilemma. Objective measurement of young children's skills and behavior may be at a time in their developmental course when they are often most unpredictable, unregulated, and uncooperative and when they often have rudimentary communication skills. Additionally, there are few assessment "gold standards" on which to base our important decisions. What procedures can we use to give us accurate information quickly? Can we rely on this test to give us a valid and reliable measurement of the child's skills so that we can plan his intervention program and assure he learns and has fun? Will this assessment help to find optimal ways to support the family with their child in the home environment?

> Whereas assessment needs to yield useful information reflecting the child's optimal skills and helping to make astute decisions about education programming, it also should be a fun, positive experience for children and families.

Jorge, the home visitor, has brought the administration kit for the standardized assessment, Bayley Scales on Infant Development, to Monica's house to assess her newborn Dan for eligibility in the local Part C early intervention program. When Jorge arrives, Dan is fussy, so Monica nurses him until he falls asleep. Jorge asks Monica several questions related to her concerns as well as general questions about Dan's skills. He tries to gently wake Dan to see if he can measure some basic developmental milestones related to eye gaze and reflexes. Dan's eyes flutter open a few times and then he closes them shut and falls into a deep sleep. Jorge has only this hour to complete the assessment, and the deadline for referral to early intervention services is imminent.

Bekka is a 4-year-old in a state prekindergarten program. Her teacher is concerned about her communication skills because she talks very little and doesn't seem to understand many general classroom instructions. With the support of Bekka's parents, her preschool teacher, Marie Rose, has requested a communication evaluation from the early childhood special education speech/language specialist. Marie Rose has asked Bekka's mother and father to meet before the assessment and to be present during the testing session. As Bekka's parents enter the preschool classroom, she runs into her father's arms, buries her head in his shoulder, and refuses to look at either her teacher or the speech/language specialist. When her parents try and get her to answer some of the assessor's questions, she buries her head even further in her father's shoulder and won't even make eye contact. She is reluctant to join snack time or other classroom activities with peers, preferring her father's lap.

The challenges of assessing young children are apparent in these scenarios. Preschool-age children often won't comply with standardized procedures, have little motivation to do well on the "test," and often don't perform well in front of people they don't know. Instead of a formal language test, if I take response data on Avril's expressive language during small group play times, I may be able to figure out what words she needs to learn so she can invite peers to play. If I collect observational data on Bernard and his same-age peers on the playground, I may be able to determine the gross-motor skills Bernard is missing so he can interact with peers on the playground.

Assessment can be particularly challenging when we attempt to measure the capabilities of children who are atypical in their development and/or have challenging behaviors. If we make mistakes or "mismeasure" children's skills, we can be misinformed about what we as parents and teachers should do, thus limiting their potential at a very young age, as learning is just beginning (Bagnato, Neisworth, & Petti-Frontczak, 2010). The repercussions of mismeasurement may be magnified over time, with potentially serious implications for the child and family.

Whereas assessment needs to yield useful information reflecting the child's optimal skills and helping to make astute decisions about education programming, it also should be a fun, positive experience for children and families. For example, we can measure Bart's jumping and balance skills when he is outside playing with a friend rather than taking him out in the hall and asking him to walk on a piece of tape on the floor. Anna's adaptive skills can be observed when she is taking her coat and boots off as she comes from the outdoors.

Assessments are often completed alone in a room (hopefully with the parent present although not always) doing "artificial" activities such as pointing to pictures in a testing book and stacking blocks in a certain shape. Currently, in some states, eligibility assessments for EI/ECSE IDEA services take more time to complete than the duration of the services the child receives once eligible, constituting a wasteful and ineffective use of scarce resource (M. Macy, Bagnato, R. S. Macy, & Salaway, 2015).

Bronfenbrenner (1979) characterized our current early childhood dilemma with his now famous statement about developmental psychology as "the science of examining the strange behaviors of children with strange adults, in strange settings for the briefest possible periods of time" (p. 19). What then can we do to mitigate this strangeness, to make sure the lenses we look through give us clear authentic images that are truly helpful for decision making?

Table 1
Principles for Developmentally Appropriate Assessment in Early Intervention/Early Childhood Special Education

Principle	Definition
Authentic	Is information on children's play and activities within everyday routines being assessed?
Acceptable	How acceptable is the assessment to parents, caregivers, providers? What is the utility of the assessment to users and families?
Collaborative	Are parents, family members, and providers involved?
Evidence-based	Is there evidence supporting the assessment for use with young children, including those with disabilities and delays?
Across Settings, Time, Methods	Are data collected across settings, caregivers, places, using different methods such as observations, interviews, direct probes?
Sensitive	Are there enough test items and are they arranged in a way to measure changes in behavior?
Universal	Can any child demonstrate strengths and limitations with adaptable items, materials?
Useful	Is the assessment linked with what the child needs to learn and his or her intervention activities?

Adapted from Bagnato, Neisworth, and Pretti-Frontczak (2010).

Authentic, Naturalistic Assessment

Many of us in the child assessment world think that the best way to solve the dilemma of early childhood assessment is by using authentic, naturalistic assessment—a developmentally appropriate alternative to conventional testing including the systematic recording of observations over time in the child's daily routines by familiar and knowledgeable caregivers, examining naturally occurring behaviors and functional competencies (Bagnato et al., 2010; Bagnato & Yeh Ho, 2006). Authentic assessment is closely related to naturalistic assessment in which multiple opportunities are provided for the child to perform naturally occurring skills across areas of development or embedded in the context of child-initiated, routine, and planned activities (Losardo & Notari-Syverson, 2011). Guiding principles for developmentally appropriate assessment in EI/ECSE are summarized in Table 1 (Bagnato et al., 2010).

What does authentic or naturalistic assessment look like for young children? First, we want caregivers, parents, and family members involved, using testing objects and procedures that are motivating for the child and are culturally relevant and conducted in the dominant language of the child/family. We want to see children's skills in their everyday environments—playing with blocks, looking at books, kicking soccer balls to friends. Ideally, we want our assessment to focus on activities that are functional, using multiple methods and strategies to yield optimal results.

Table 2
Assessment Properties

Validity	Does the assessment measure what it says it measures? Was a broad normative sample recruited that is similar to the children/families with whom the test will be used?
Reliability	Are the results consistent across people, time?
Utility	Is the test easy to use? Are the materials attractive to and appropriate for the child? Are procedures clear and training easy to access? Are results easy for family members to understand?
Sociocultural competence	Does the test elicit and assess skills in a broad, multifaceted way that includes all children/families (Losardo & Notari-Syverson, 2011)?

Valid, Reliable, Culturally Competent Assessments

To assure that assessments provide us with accurate, appropriate, and effective information for our decision making, we must choose tools with established and acceptable assessment properties, tests that have been studied and have evidence supporting their use (Snow & Van Hemel, 2008). Foremost among these assessment properties are validity, reliability, utility, and sociocultural competence (see Table 2).

Assessment Processes

Generally in EI/ECSE, assessments for young children are used in one of four processes: screening, eligibility, educational planning, and evaluation (Bricker & Littman, 1982; McLean, Hemmeter, & Snyder, 2014). In each process, or for each decision to be made, a specific type of assessment tool is usually used. The major processes, questions answered, and types of assessment are described in Table 3, including examples of each type of assessment.

Typically, these four assessment processes and associated measures make up an "assessment system" in EI/ECSE. Figure 1 includes an ideal, linked approach to EI/ECSE assessment and instruction (Bagnato et al., 2010; Bricker & Littman, 1982). In a linked system (see Figure 1), information from each process is tied or linked to the next process, and information collected during one process can inform decisions made in the next phase. Each assessment process is described below.

Screening is a brief, formal evaluation of skills intended to identify those children with potential problems who should be referred for a more in-depth

Table 3
Assessment Processes and Tools

Process	Question	Type of Assessment	Examples
Screening	Is further testing needed? Is focused teaching needed (universal screening)?	Norm referenced, standardized Judgment based; general outcome measures	Ages & Stages Questionnaires (Squires & Bricker, 2009), Brigance Early Childhood Screens (Brigance, 2013), Kindergarten and Preschool Behavior Scales-2 (Merrell, 2002)
Eligibility/ diagnostic	Does the child qualify for specialized services? What is the nature of his or her delay?	Norm referenced, standardized	Bayley Scales of Infant Development (Bayley, 2005), Mullen Scales of Early Learning (Mullen, 1995), Preschool Language Scales (Zimmerman, Steiner, & Pond, 2011)
Educational planning	What is the child's current skill level? What are the best supports and strategies?	Curriculum-based	Assessment, Evaluation Programming System (Bricker, 2002), Creative Curriculum for Infants and Toddlers, & Twos (Dodge, Rudick, & Berke, 2006), HighScope Child Observation Record (HighScope Educational Research Foundation, 1992)
Evaluation	Is the child making progress? Is the classroom making progress toward goals and objectives?	Curriculum-based	Assessment, Evaluation Programming System (Bricker, 2002), Carolina Curriculum (Johnson-Martin, Attermeier, & Hacker, 2004), Dynamic Indicators of Basic Early Literacy Skills (DIBELS) (Good & Kaminski, 1996)

assessment. Screening instruments are usually quick, easy to administer, and should be supported by studies confirming their validity and reliability. Screening in the early childhood years can include broad developmental screening measures (Ages & Stages Questionnaires and Brigance Early Childhood Screens), domain specific tests (Peabody Developmental Motor Scales, MacArthur-Bates Communicative Development Inventory), and social-emotional/behavioral assessments (Brief Infant Toddler Social Emotional Assessment, Early Screening Inventory) as well as tests focused on sensory functions such as hearing and vision. Many screening assessments can be administered in multiple authentic environments, including childcare centers, preschool classes, and in the home. Simple screening tools, often completed by parents and caregivers, can be administered at minimal cost and with valuable input from caregivers who know the child well. Developmental screening of all young children is a recommended strategy for improving

Figure 1
Linked Systems Model for Assessment

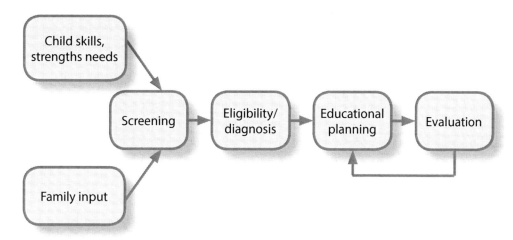

outcomes through identification of delays and disabilities at the earliest point possible (Bricker, Macy, et al., 2012; Technical Assistance Center on Social Emotional Intervention for Young Children, n.d.).

Screening assessments usually yield three outcomes: typical, at risk needs further evaluation, and questionable and needs further monitoring. Children needing further evaluation can be referred to a developmental/behavioral specialist and/or to an EI/ECSE eligibility team that will complete further testing and information gathering to determine whether the child is eligible for IDEA services. Children whose developmental status is questionable or difficult to determine can be referred for further assessment if parents and practitioners think more assistance and supports are needed, or they can be monitored at frequent intervals to make sure their development is on track. Prevention activities targeting developmental/behavioral needs can be given to parents, teachers, and caregivers. Children should be screened periodically through their first five years to assure their developmental course is on track (Squires, Bricker, & Twombly, 2015).

The **eligibility/diagnostic** assessment process that follows screening usually includes standardized norm-referenced tests to determine the nature of a child's delays and eligibility for EI/ECSE services as well as programs or other community supports that might be warranted, such as behavioral consulting, parent support, and mental health counseling. Standardized norm-referenced tests were first developed for use with adults and often do not fit the behavioral and developmental realities of young children (Bagnato, 2007). In addition, standardized norm-referenced assessments often require extensive professional time and do not yield information that is helpful for intervention programs that will be working with the child and family on a daily basis (Johnson, Rahn, & Bricker, 2015). Although most state IDEA eligibility guidelines require standardized assessments, many states are accepting more naturalistic, authentic assessments of children in their everyday environment (Bagnato, 2007; Bricker, Yovanoff, Capt, & Allen, 2003).

Standardized norm-referenced measures include eligibility and diagnostic

> Screening assessments usually yield three outcomes: typical, at risk needs further evaluation, and questionable and needs further monitoring.

assessments described above in Table 3, such as the Bayley Scales of Infant Development (Bayley, 2005) and the Battelle Developmental Inventory (Newborg, 2004) that assist in determining whether a child exhibits a significant delay and thus is eligible for services as well as pinpointing the nature of the disability (e.g., autism spectrum disorder). As mentioned above, these tests are often completed in one session with a child, eliciting activities that delineate individual child skills but are time consuming and often do not yield information useful for educational planning.

After eligibility is determined, the next assessment process is **educational planning**. Curriculum-based measures (CBMs) are used for this process, yielding results about how children are performing on expected criteria. CBMs map a child's achievements on a series of skills, usually arranged in developmental order. They contain a sequence of developmental objectives, sometimes called learning or general outcomes. For example, items related to gross-motor skills such as walking and hopping, adaptive skills such as eating and dressing, and social skills such as playing with peers and sharing toys are included in a developmental hierarchy. CBMs produce outcomes that are directly applicable to what the child needs to learn and allow for assessing children at short as well as more long-term intervals, such as quarterly to see what tasks and/or developmental skills they have mastered. These outcomes are usually the long-range goals of a curriculum and include suggested activities in a sequence of finely graded skills. CBMs allow for pinpointing a child's learning style as well as targeting teaching objectives and providing examples of activities that encourage these skills and are used for developing IFSPs or IEPs and for revising these plans when necessary.

CBMs, described above in Table 3, include curriculum items with specific performance criteria that are linked to and aligned with what is being taught. CBMs are particularly well suited for use with young children with disabilities because they are adaptable for skill levels, naturalistic or authentic, and are valuable for developing IFSPs/IEPs, educational planning, and evaluation of child and program progress.

Evaluation is the final assessment process that measures a child's (or program's) progress over time. Evaluation of child's progress often includes a child's results on a CBM, such as whether they have met their long-term motor goal of walking without assistance. Evaluation can also include assessing an entire classroom on meeting specific learning standards, such as the percent of children who can work at a task independently for 10 minutes, as well as making judgments about whether an entire program is achieving its goals, such as being ready to transition to the next learning environment. Evaluation of child or classroom progress is often based on CBM results as well as portfolios, parent surveys, and ongoing observations, which are described below.

Renaldo, age 2½, was referred to the Desert Early Service Program after a screening test at the pediatrician's office indicated potential delays in communication and gross-motor areas. The early intervention assessment team asked Renaldo and his father, Wendell, to come to the toddler classroom at the local preschool program. Teacher Tiffani asked Renaldo and Wendell if they would sit at the snack table and have some juice and snacks while Wendell answered some questions.

> Observational instruments, another kind of assessment, focus on children in their natural environments and often assign ratings or numerical values to behaviors.

The speech language specialist, Monica, joined them at the table to record a language sample. Tiffani asked Renaldo if he wanted crackers, raisins, or cheese. He looked at his father, and Wendell encouraged him to tell Tiffani what he wanted. He first pointed to crackers and raisins, and his father again encouraged him to use his words. He made some sound approximations (crac-cac and way), and Tiffani gave him some of each food. She also offered a snack and juice to Wendell.

After they finished eating, Tiffani encouraged Renaldo to clean up his snack plate and choose a toy from the shelf. He followed these directions without a problem and chose the large Lego set. Tiffani asked Wendell to give Renaldo Legos that would require snapping on and off to get a sense of his fine-motor skills. After playing for 10 minutes, they went outside to the play area, and Tiffani asked Wendell to have Renaldo do some gross-motor skills such as jumping, running, and throwing a ball. The speech language specialist followed Renaldo outside and continued to assess his language, asking Wendell to have Renaldo use certain language such as combining words to make sentences, asking for a big or small ball, and asking whether he was in the blue or red swing.

After 15 minutes outside, Renaldo and Wendell went back inside and continued playing using classroom toys until data had been taken on expressive and receptive language, gross- and fine-motor skills, and adaptive skills. Using these data, the Vineland Interview, and a standardized parent questionnaire, the MacArthur-Bates Communicative Development Inventories (Fenson et al., 2006), the team met after this visit and agreed that Renaldo was eligible for EI services. They asked Renaldo and Wendell to return the following week for an additional play session to complete items on the Carolina Infant and Toddler Curriculum (Johnson-Martin et al., 2004) to identify additional learning goals and objectives.

In this scenario, Renaldo's eligibility assessment was completed in a naturalistic and family-friendly way, with Renaldo playing and completing everyday activities, while at the same time completing tasks on several standardized assessments and parent interviews. Data were completed across settings and materials with the help and direction of Renaldo's father. In addition, initial information about educational planning was gathered during the eligibility assessment.

Observational instruments, another kind of assessment, focus on children in their natural environments and often assign ratings or numerical values to behaviors. For example, the PICCOLO rates caregiver-child interactions in terms of responsiveness of parent-to-child communication, positive affect, and parent encouragement of child engagement (Cook & Roggman, 2009; Roggman,

Cook, Innocenti, Jump, & Christiansen, 2013). The Child Behavior Checklist (Achenbach & Rescorla, 2000) asks parents or teachers to rate a child's problem behaviors, asking questions such as whether the child is "disturbed by any change in routine" or "wants a lot of attention."

Observational data also can be gathered by teachers on children's behaviors, such as calculating the percent of on-task behavior during group activities, the quality and quantity of interactions with peers outdoors, and the time it takes for a child to join group circle time. At home, parents can collect observational data on skills such as their child's eating and sleeping behaviors, ability to dress self before school, and frequency and number of two-word sentences. Observations can provide critical data to assist in the decision-making processes.

Functional behavior assessment (FBA) includes specific procedures for observing behaviors that may be hampering learning. FBAs are useful in identifying the causes of challenging behavior and assisting intervention plans for decreasing these behaviors, based on their form and function. For example, if Neena acts out by screaming to get out of participating in circle time, how might the task of attending circle be modified so her participation is less aversive? FBA includes a collection of processes to identify problem behavior, determine the reason or function of the behavior, and develop alternative actions for Neena to use when she needs a break (Benedict, Horner, & Squires, 2007; Squires & Bricker, 2007).

Portfolio assessments include documenting a child's progress using authentic products and descriptions of behavior in the child's everyday environments. A portfolio assessment is based on process and evaluation criteria, usually with the involvement of the child and family. Portfolios include selections focused on the assessment question, usually a collection of the child's products, videos, schedules, etc. For example, a child's self-portraits might be collected over time to evaluate self-image and social-emotional growth. Portfolio assessments are particularly valuable when assessing children with significant delays whose growth may not be measured well by existing assessment tools. Formal portfolio assessments include the Ounce Scale (Meisels, Marsden, Dombro, Weston, & Jewkes, 2003) and the Work Sampling System (Meisels, Marsden, Jablon, Dorfman, & Dichtelmiller, 2001).

Rating scales include judging whether a child has certain skills or behaviors and to what extent they display these behaviors. Rating scales often focus on a child's performance on specified behaviors, usually rated on a 1–4 or 1–5 Likert scale. Kindergarten assessments often include rating scales, with items such as "child knows 75% of beginning sounds" or "child observes rules and follows directions without reminders." In early childhood settings, rating scales focused on environmental supports and structures are also widely used, such as the Infant/Toddler Environmental Rating Scale (Harms, Cryer, & Clifford, 2006) and the Pre-School SET (Steed, Pomerleau, & Horner, 2012). Finally, assessments of social-emotional and behavioral competence are often rating scales, asking parents and providers to rate the frequency of behaviors on a Likert scale, such as *rarely or never* to *most of the time*. Examples of behavioral rating scales include the Child Behavior Checklist (Achenbach & Rescorla, 2000), Behavior Assessment Scale for Children (Reynolds & Kamphaus, 2004), and the Pediatric Symptom Checklist (Jellinek & Murphy, 1998).

Interviews are a final example of naturalistic assessments. Interviews with parents, teachers, siblings, and the child can yield important information about a child's preferences, daily routines, and functional skills (McWilliam, 2010). Interviews may fall in one of the main assessment process categories shown in Table 3 or may be informal and used for clarifying any additional information gathered during the assessment process. For example, the Vineland Adaptive Behavior Scale (Sparrow, Cicchetti, & Balla, 2008) is a standardized norm-referenced assessment based on interviewing parents/caregivers to determine eligibility for EI/ECSE services. Interviewing parents on daily routines and possible schedules for embedding learning opportunities (McWilliam, 2010) is a second example.

Whatever the assessment approach, the gathering of information must match the purpose and questions that need to be answered about the child and must fit parent and practitioner needs as well as those of a general audience or stakeholders. In addition, approaches must be evidence-based—have empirical support gathered about their validity and reliability—to assure that they are accurate and provide useful information for making important decisions.

Empirical Support for DEC Recommended Assessment Practices

Research-based practices are those that have been demonstrated to be effective and are supported by evidence reported in the research literature (Odom et al., 2005). A major difficulty in identifying research-based evidence to support these assessment practices with children with delays and disabilities is that the population of young children with and at risk for disabilities is extremely heterogeneous and few in numbers. This makes conducting experimental designs very challenging. For example, young children with Down syndrome, even at exactly the same age, vary widely in terms of developmental skills, physical characteristics, social-emotional skills, and cognitive ability. The same is true of children who experience a cognitive delay; some may have minimal limitations and others may have co-occurring social-emotional and/or language difficulties that make completing standardized tasks difficult. Thus designing studies with equivalent groups is difficult, limiting both quasi and randomized group studies that might be used as supportive evidence.

A second difficulty with empirical evidence, mentioned above, is that the procedures, items, and processes associated with standardized assessments—the most often used outcome measures in empirical studies—are often a poor match for the EI/ECSE population. Each child with a delay or disability is unique and as such may have specific limitations prohibiting answering test items within

> Whatever the assessment approach, the gathering of information must match the purpose and questions that need to be answered about the child and must fit parent and practitioner needs as well as those of a general audience or stakeholders.

a certain time frame or using specific materials, which may be of little interest or difficult to manipulate. Indeed, for children with visual, motor, and language delays, the very means by which standardized "intelligence" is measured (e.g., looking at picture cards, pointing to objects, walking in a straight line) may be prohibited because of the nature of their delay, not because of cognitive limitations. In addition, children with disabilities often are not included in studies undertaken when gathering evidence to support the validity of an assessment, making it difficult to generalize outcomes to this population.

To the extent possible, the evidence base for these recommended practices comes from studies that meet the following criteria: (1) follow methodologically sound and high-quality designs (randomized control group, quasi-experimental, and/or single subject); (2) are reported in the research literature, published in peer-review journals, and replicated by a variety of researchers and research teams; and (3) demonstrate positive effects on specific child or family outcomes. We searched a variety of literature in a wide range of fields—psychology, early childhood, EI/ECSE, education, special education, pediatrics, and behavioral medicine—to find specific studies that provided direct empirical support drawn from high-quality studies. For example, we want parents involved in the assessment process because we know parental involvement usually yields better outcomes (Shonkoff, 2010) and it is mandated by IDEA (2004). We found qualitative and narrative evidence (Crais, Roy, & Free, 2006; Farrell, O'Sullivan, & Quinn, 2009), yet finding specific studies focused on empirical benefits of family involvement in the assessment process was difficult.

As a second example, we know that linked assessment and evaluation processes in a program are more efficient in terms of gathering and using assessment information because the same tools are often used in multiple processes. When using the linked assessment and evaluation processes, the focus stays on the skills targeted by the assessment rather than related skills or measurement approaches that may magnify measurement error (Bagnato et al., 2010; Bell, Corfield, Davies, & Richardson, 2010; Johnson et al., 2015). Finally, we know that naturalistic approaches that collect data throughout the child's day and settings—rather than during one trial in a small clinical office—provide multiple opportunities for the child to display target skills as well as a more accurate measuring of those skills (Keilty, LaRocoo, & Casell, 2009). We did not find specific studies comparing naturalistic assessment approaches vs. standardized scripted approaches; however, we found related studies comparing naturalistic and teacher-directed intervention approaches (Losardo & Bricker, 1994; Rule, Losardo, Dinnebeil, Kaiser, & Rowland, 1998).

Except for a few instances, standardized assessments themselves have not been studied vis-à-vis the EI/ECSE eligibility process (Macy et al., 2015). Macy et al. (2015) found only 44 studies exploring the technical adequacy of conventional standardized assessments in the EI eligibility process. Their conclusions stated that there are "serious questions about the lack of critical qualities, field validation, and evidence base of conventional tests and testing to fulfill the purpose of early intervention eligibility determination" (p. 182).

Standardized test developers, including those associated with the Bayley Scales and the Battelle Developmental Inventory, have attempted to make testing

> Practitioners, researchers, and administrators need to take these recommendations to the next step. Use them, discuss them with families and other service providers, and find where the practices work and where you think they need further discussion or modification.

procedures more flexible and culturally appropriate for young children with and at risk for disabilities. However, a contradiction exists because universal design modifications that may better fit the needs of children with disabilities cannot be used when adhering to standardized testing and scoring protocols most often used in eligibility assessments.

We in EI/ECSE then need to be creative, sensitive, and thoughtful when using conventional standardized tests and hopefully combine results from a variety of sources and approaches to make accurate and timely eligibility decisions. Often, for very young children and families, especially children with diverse needs and limited skills, we may need to "stretch" the function of tests to make the assessment process work for children and families (Bricker, Squires, & Clifford, 2010). For example, curriculum-based assessments are accepted in many states as a second measure for determining EI/ECSE eligibility. Many nonverbal children may be able to complete multiple tasks on curriculum-based assessments that give information about their motor, cognitive, adaptive, and language skills that are not elicited by items on standardized tests such as the Bayley Scales.

We also need to use linked or additive assessment processes to enhance our information gathering efforts. For example, if during the screening process Rosita displays only a few fine-motor skills, arranging for a motor assessment by a physical therapist as well as giving her items from a CBM within her general developmental level may help with determining eligibility as well as steer instructional programming in motor and other domains.

The Recommended Practices

Eleven practices related to assessment are included in these recommendations. Key to these are a family focus, sociocultural competence, and inclusion of information from the family collected at home and in the community throughout the assessment process. Also suggested is a systematic approach that begins with screening, followed by determining eligibility, planning for educational activities, monitoring child progress, and finally measuring child and program outcomes. Emphasis is also put on blending assessment approaches, using multiple methods, and focusing on the child's strengths, preferences, and interests. Finally, it's important to discuss assessment results with families and other practitioners using easily understandable and useful language.

Practitioners, researchers, and administrators need to take these recommendations to the next step. Use them, discuss them with families and other service providers, and find where the practices work and where you think they need further discussion or modification. For researchers, there are tremendous opportunities to gather empirical evidence on these standards. Despite the difficulties with research in this area, it is incumbent upon researchers and practitioners to gather data and feedback and continue to modify and refine these practices to assure that the assessment process includes accurate and useful assessment information that helps us inform the educational process and produces optimal outcomes for children and families.

References

Achenbach, T., & Rescorla, L. (2000). *Child behavior checklist (CBCL)*. Burlington: University of Vermont Department of Psychiatry.

Bagnato, S. J. (2007). *Authentic assessment for early childhood intervention: Best practices*. New York, NY: Guilford Press.

Bagnato, S. J., Neisworth, J. T., & Pretti-Frontczak, K. (2010). *Linking authentic assessment and early childhood intervention: Best measures for best practices* (2nd ed.). Baltimore, MD: Paul H. Brookes.

Bagnato, S. J., & Yeh Ho, H. (2006). High stakes testing with preschool children: Violation of professional standards for evidence based practice in early childhood intervention. *KEDI Journal of Educational Policy, 3*(1), 23–43.

Bayley, N. (2005). *Bayley scales of infant development* (3rd ed.). San Antonio, TX: Pearson.

Bell, A., Corfield, M., Davies, J., & Richardson, N. (2010). Collaborative transdisciplinary intervention in early years – putting theory into practice. *Child: Care, Health and Development, 36*, 142–148. doi:10.1111/j.1365-2214.2009.01027.x

Benedict, E. A., Horner, R. H., & Squires, J. K. (2007). Assessment and implementation of positive behavior support in preschools. *Topics in Early Childhood Special Education, 27*, 174–192. doi:10.1177/02711214070270030801

Bricker, D. (2002). *Assessment, evaluation, and programming system for infants and children* (2nd ed., Vols. 1–4). Baltimore, MD: Paul H. Brookes.

Bricker, D., & Littman, D. (1982). Intervention and evaluation: The inseparable mix. *Topics in Early Childhood Special Education, 1*(4), 23–33. doi:10.1177/027112148200100407

Bricker, D., Macy, M., Squires, J., & Marks, K. (2013). *Developmental screening in your community: An integrated approach for connecting children with services*. Baltimore, MD: Paul H. Brookes.

Bricker, D., Squires, J., & Clifford, J. (2010). Developmental screening measures: Stretching the use of the ASQ for other assessment purposes. *Infants & Young Children, 23*, 14–22. doi:10.1097/IYC.0b013e3181c816cc

Bricker, D., Yovanoff, R., Capt, B., & Allen, D. (2003). Use of a curriculum-based measure to corroborate eligibility decisions. *Journal of Early Intervention, 26*, 20–30. doi:10.1177/105381510302600102

Brigance, A. (2013). *Brigance early childhood screens* (3rd ed.). North Billerica, MA: Curriculum Associates.

Bronfenbrenner, U. (1979). *The ecology of human development: Experiments by nature and design*. Cambridge, MA: Harvard University Press.

Cook, G. A., & Roggman, L. A. (2009, January). *PICCOLO – Parenting interactions with children: Checklist of observations linked to outcomes* (Technical report). Logan: Utah State University.

Crais, E. R., Roy, V. P., & Free, K. (2006). Parents' and professionals' perceptions of the implementation of family-centered practices in child assessments. *American Journal of Speech-Language Pathology, 15,* 365–377. doi:10.1044/1058-0360(2006/034)

Dodge, D. T., Rudick, S., & Berke, K.-L. (2006). *Creative curriculum for infants, toddlers, & twos* (2nd ed.). Washington DC: Teaching Strategies.

Farrell, A. F., O'Sullivan, C., & Quinn, L. (2009). Parent perspectives on early childhood assessment: A focus group inquiry. *Early Childhood Services, 3*(1), 61–76.

Fenson, L., Marchman, V. A., Thai, D. J., Dale, P. S., Reznick, J. S., & Bates, E. (2006). *MacArthur-Bates communicative development inventories: User's guide and technical manual* (2nd ed.). Baltimore, MD: Paul H. Brookes.

Good, R. H., & Kaminski, R. A. (1996). Assessment for instructional decisions: Toward a proactive/prevention model of decision-making for early literacy skills. *School Psychology Quarterly, 11,* 326–336. doi:10.1037/h0088938

Harms, T., Cryer, D., & Clifford, R. M. (2006). *Infant/toddler environment rating scale* (Rev. ed.). New York, NY: Teachers College Press.

HighScope Educational Research Foundation. (1992). *HighScope child observation record: For ages 2½–6*. Ypsilanti, MI: HighScope Press.

Individuals with Disabilities Education Act, 20 U.S.C. § 1400 (2004).

Jellinek, M., & Murphy, M. (1998). *Pediatric symptom checklist*. St. Paul: Minnesota Department of Health. Retrieved from http://www.health.state.mn.us/divs/fh/mch/devscrn/instr/psc.html

Johnson, J., Rahn, N. L. & Bricker, D. (2015). *An activity-based approach to early intervention* (4th ed.). Baltimore, MD: Paul H. Brookes.

Johnson-Martin, M. M., Attermeier, S. M., & Hacker, B. J. (2004). *The Carolina curriculum for infants and toddlers with special needs* (3rd ed.). Baltimore, MD: Paul H. Brookes.

Keilty, B., LaRocco, D. J., & Casell, F. B. (2009). Early interventionists' reports of authentic assessment methods through focus group research. *Topics in Early Childhood Special Education, 28,* 244–256. doi:10.1177/0271121408327477

Losardo. A., & Bricker, D. (1994). Activity-based intervention and direct instruction: A comparison study. *American Journal on Mental Retardation, 98,* 744–765.

Losardo, A., & Notari-Syverson, A. (2011). *Alternative approaches to assessing young children* (2nd ed.). Baltimore, MD: Paul H. Brookes.

Macy, M., Bagnato, S. J., Macy, R. S., & Salaway, J. (2015). Conventional tests and testing for early intervention eligibility: Is there an evidence base? *Infants & Young Children, 28,* 182–204. doi:10.1097/IYC.0000000000000032

McLean, M. E., Hemmeter, M. L., & Snyder, P. (2014). *Essential elements for assessing infants and preschoolers with special needs*. Old Tappan, NJ: Pearson.

McWilliam, R. A. (2010). *Routines-based early intervention: Supporting young children and their families*. Baltimore, MD: Paul H. Brookes.

Meisels, S. J., Marsden, D. B., Dombro, A. L., Weston, D. R., & Jewkes, A. M. (2003). *The ounce scale*. New York, NY: Pearson Early Learning.

Meisels, S. J., Marsden, D. B., Jablon, J. R., Dorfman, A. B., & Dichtelmiller, M. L. (2001). *The work sampling system* (4th ed.). New York, NY: Pearson Early Learning.

Merrell, K. W. (2002). *Preschool and kindergarten behavior scales* (2nd ed.). Austin, TX: PRO-ED

Mullen, E. M. (1995). *Mullen scales of early learning*. Circle Pines, MN: American Guidance Service.

Newborg, J. (2004). *Battelle developmental inventory* (2nd ed.). Itasca, IL: Riverside.

Odom, S. L., Brantlinger, E., Gersten, R., Horner, R. H., Thompson, B., & Harris, K. R. (2005). Research in special education: Scientific methods and evidenced-based practices. *Exceptional Children, 71*, 137–148. doi:10.1177/001440290507100201

Reynolds, C. R., & Kamphaus, R. W. (2004). *Behavior assessment for children* (2nd ed.). Toronto, ON: Pearson.

Roggman, L. A., Cook, G. A., Innocenti, M. S., Jump, V. N., & Christiansen, K. (2013). Parenting interactions with children: Checklist of observations linked to outcomes (PICCOLO) in diverse ethnic groups. *Infant Mental Health Journal, 34*, 290–306. doi:10.1002/imhj.21389

Rule, S., Losardo, A., Dinnebeil, L., Kaiser, A., & Rowland, C. (1998). Translating research on naturalistic instruction into practice. *Journal of Early Intervention, 21*, 283–293. doi:10.1177/105381519802100401

Shonkoff, J. P. (2010). Building a new biodevelopment framework to guide the future of early childhood policy. *Child Development, 81*, 357–367. doi:10.1111/j.1467-8624.2009.01399.x

Snow, C. E., & Van Hemel, S. B. (2008). *Early childhood assessment: Why, what and how*. Washington, DC: National Academies Press.

Sparrow, S. S., Cicchetti, D. V., & Balla, D. A. (2005). *Vineland adaptive behavior scales* (2nd ed.).Circle Pines, MN: American Guidance Service.

Squires, J., & Bricker, D. (2007). *An activity-based approach to developing young children's social and emotional competence*. Baltimore, MD: Paul H. Brookes.

Squires, J., & Bricker, D. (2009). *Ages & stages questionnaires user's guide: A parent-completed child-monitoring system* (3rd ed.). Baltimore, MD: Paul H. Brookes.

Squires, J., Bricker, D., & Twombly, E. (2015). *Ages & stages questionnaires: Social-emotional* (2nd ed.). Baltimore, MD: Paul H. Brookes.

Steed, E. A., Pomerleau, T. M., & Horner, R. H. (2012). *Preschool-wide evaluation tool, research edition*. Baltimore, MD: Paul H. Brookes.

Technical Assistance Center on Social Emotional Intervention for Young Children. (n.d.). Retrieved from http://challengingbehavior.fmhi.usf.edu/

Zimmerman, I. L., Steiner, V. G., & Pond, R. E. (2011). *Preschool language scales* (5th ed.). San Antonio, TX: Pearson.

5

ENVIRONMENT

Improving Access and Participation

TRICIA CATALINO
Touro University Nevada

LORI E. MEYER
University of Vermont

ENVIRONMENT INFLUENCES THE HEALTH AND DEVELOPMENT OF ALL children, especially young children who have or are at risk for developmental delays or disabilities. For more than 30 years, Bronfenbrenner's (1979) ecological theory of human development has guided our understanding of the role environments have in children's development. Early childhood intervention researchers have applied this theory to advance our understanding of environmental influence on the development of young children. For those who have or are at risk for developmental delays or disabilities and their families, Bronfenbrenner's ecological theory has addressed many pressing issues in early childhood intervention. These include the implementation of inclusive education (Odom, 2002), family-centered services (Bruder, 2000), and natural learning opportunities (Dunst et al., 2001), to name just a few.

In this introduction to the Division for Early Childhood (DEC) Recommended Practices, we will briefly explain what we mean by the environment and what it means for young children with disabilities and their families. This will provide a framework for conceptualizing the inter-relatedness of environmental settings and features. We will also define types of environments in which children develop and grow and outline key ideas to consider when implementing the Environment recommended practices. This article will use vignettes to illustrate important themes and show examples of how practitioners can best use the Environment recommended practices.

While exploring the nuances of Bronfenbrenner's ecological theory may be beyond the scope of this article, we believe it fitting to introduce the new topic area of the Environment recommended practices with a nod to the theory that has given our field a lens for understanding the complex world of supporting positive outcomes for young children with disabilities and their families. We also believe it is important to celebrate the work of the Environment workgroup members who wrote and advised on practices for this topic area. Our deep appreciation and gratitude goes to Kaitlin Bargreen, Bill Brown, Deborah Cassidy, Robyn Ridgely, Eleni Soukakou, and their leader, Rena Hallam.

Evolution of Environment Recommended Practices From 2005 to 2014

The Environment recommended practices is a new and important topic area in the most recent update of the recommended practices (Division for Early Childhood, 2014); however, this was not the first time it was considered. Environment was proposed and investigated as a strand in 1998, and while not a standalone strand at that time, the 2005 DEC Recommended Practices (Sandall, Hemmeter, Smith & McLean, 2005) did note their presence. More specifically, a number of child-focused practices addressed the learning environment's role in early childhood intervention practices.

The Recommended Practices Commission, charged by the DEC Executive Board to make sure the newly revised practices reflect contemporary thinking, decided to bolster the prominence of the environment in the new recommended practices by creating a separate topic area to match the attention environmental quality has had in our field over the last decade (Campbell & Milbourne, 2014). With this line of thinking, the commission asked the Environment workgroup to identify specific practices that enhanced aspects of the physical space, materials, routines, and activities that provide context for children's learning and social interactions with adults and peers. Additionally, as is true for the other recommended practices, the goal was to create practices that extended the National Association for the Education of Young Children's (NAEYC) Developmentally Appropriate Practices (DAPs) across the age span from birth to age 8.

> Environmental settings and features are inseparably linked to young children's development, growth, and functioning.

Building Upon Developmentally Appropriate Environment Practices

Research-based evidence and experiential wisdom has helped explain how DAPs influence young children's development with consideration of their age and social/cultural contexts (Copple & Bredekamp, 2009). To determine how to expand on DAPs for the Environment recommended practices, the guiding question was "What should practitioners do when environments do not support the access and participation of young children with disabilities?" The joint position statement on inclusion, collaboratively written by DEC and NAEYC (2009), helped formulate this question. Additionally, we sought to have Environment practices that would promote access and participation of all children, especially young children with or at risk for developmental delays or disabilities, and would consider environment an intervention strategy.

Together, the Environment recommended practices guide practitioners to take action that may not be automatic or intuitive when creating developmentally appropriate early care and education settings. Because the Environment

Table 1
Examples of How Environment DEC Recommended Practices Build Upon DAPs

Developmentally Appropriate Practice	Environment DEC RP	What should practitioners do when environments do not support the access and participation of young children with disabilities?
Caregivers carefully arrange the visual environment with things that are interesting to look at from an infant's perspective.	E3	For an infant with a visual impairment … It may be necessary to modify the physical environment by displaying a few, bright, shiny materials/toys on a neutral colored shelf.
Caregivers provide toddlers with utensils that they can easily use.	E5	For a toddler with fine-motor delays … It may be necessary to use utensils with different-shaped handles that allow the toddler to participate in meals and snacks as independently as possible.
Teachers encourage preschoolers' healthy habits in exercise.	E6	For a preschooler with gross-motor delays … It may be necessary to provide incentives for movement such as having the preschooler identify classroom friends to play with during a favorite movement game outside (e.g., red light, green light).

Note: Developmentally appropriate practice examples are adapted from Copple and Bredekamp (2009).

recommended practices build upon DAPs, they lead to the creation of environments that would be beneficial for all young children—and imperative for young children with disabilities (see Table 1 for examples of how this can work for practitioners in the field).

Conceptualizing Environments in the DEC Recommended Practices

It cannot be overstated that inherent to all of the recommended practices, including those under Environment, is the prominence of natural and inclusive environments (Division for Early Childhood, 2014). Environments, as described in this article and in the DEC Recommended Practices, refers to both environmental settings (e.g., inclusive and natural) and environmental features (e.g., physical, social, and temporal). Conceptualizing environments in this way highlights how environmental settings and features are inseparably linked to young children's development, growth, and functioning. Furthermore, it calls attention to the role environments have in supporting positive outcomes for young children who have or are at risk for developmental delays and disabilities.

To further illustrate the relationship between the different environments embedded in the Environment recommended practices, we propose a conceptual framework (see Figure 1) that builds on previous work by Kolobe, Arevalo, and

Figure 1
Conceptual Framework of Inter-related Environmental Factors That Affect Child Outcomes and Participation

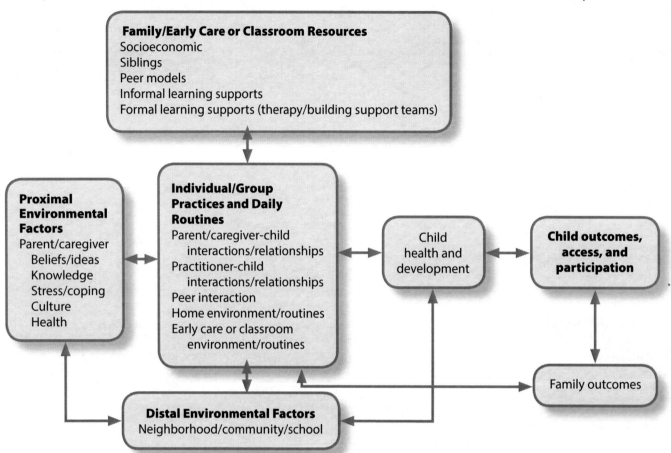

Note: Adapted from Kolobe, T. H., Arevalo, A., & Catalino, T. A. (2012). The environment of intervention. In S. K. Campbell, R. J. Palisano, & M. N. Orlin (Eds.), *Physical therapy for children* (4th ed., pp. 879–902). St. Louis, MO: Elsevier.

Catalino (2012) to show the relationship of proximal (home/family) and distal (neighborhood, community, school) environmental factors that influence child outcomes and participation. The Environment recommended practices are integrated in the framework in areas where practitioners can most likely use their knowledge and skills to help increase access to and participation in learning opportunities for children. For example, recommended practice E1 aligns with both intrinsic family factors and child-rearing practices/daily routines because the practitioner provides services in natural and inclusive environments during daily routines and activities. Family and classroom resources align with all of the Environment practices, and the neighborhood, community, and school align with E2 and E6, where the physical environment can either facilitate or inhibit opportunities for access to public space and activities. Please refer to Division for Early Childhood (2014) for a complete list of the Environment recommended practices (E1–E6).

Interconnection of Environmental Features

Because of the multiplicity of environmental features, practitioners must be prepared to implement modifications and adaptations that support children and families in natural and inclusive environments while optimizing children's function and participation. It is important to remember that no one environmental feature stands alone. This means that modifying or adapting any feature from one type of environment to support children's learning and development may influence another environment and/or other related learning goals. Examples of this interconnection are provided in the following two vignettes:

Erin is a physical therapist who works with a family and their infant son, Kyle, who has Down syndrome. Kyle's mother, Cindy, would like to have "tummy time" with him because she used this practice with both his siblings when they were young. Yet, Cindy is worried that Kyle's siblings might be too rough around him if she places him on the floor. Erin was sensitive to Cindy's concerns and worked with her to create a safe space in the living room for Kyle's tummy time.

Daniel is a speech/language pathologist in an early childhood special education classroom, where he supports Gabriella, a 4-year-old with cerebral palsy. He noticed that Gabriella is very motivated by her classmates, but during meal time she has difficulty managing the cup and utensils, so often she does not finish her food. Daniel works closely with the teacher and an occupational therapist to modify utensils and a straw cup to help Gabriella eat and drink more easily alongside her classmates.

These two examples address the physical environment; however, such modifications are likely to influence the social and temporal environments as well. In the tummy time example, the physical therapist also will have to consider the infant's schedule (temporal environment) and the family's beliefs, culture, and values around child-rearing to make tummy time an engaging and productive activity for both the infant *and* the family (social environment). Likewise, in the meal-time example, the therapists and teacher must consider the classroom schedule and time required to eat (temporal environment) while promoting socialization with peers at the table (social environment). In this case, participation is not only about independence with eating and drinking but also about being a full member of the classroom community.

The Spirit of the Environment Recommended Practices

As in other formal documents, the DEC Recommended Practices can be interpreted both literally and from the perspectives of those who meticulously wrote and revised them. This latter interpretation is sometimes implicit, passed on by word of mouth and substantiated as practitioners, educators, and researchers use the practices in the field and share their experiences. It is our intention to put forth three key ideas to aid users of the Environment recommended practices to understand the spirit in which they were established and to supplement information already available in the DEC Recommended Practices.

(1) Environmental practices are interwoven within all DEC RP areas. As mentioned, different types of environments are inseparably linked. To build on this idea, the different types of environments also are woven through the six other topic areas in the recommended practices. It is impossible to separate the

> It is important to remember that no one environmental feature stands alone. This means that modifying or adapting any feature from one type of environment to support children's learning and development may influence another environment and/or other related learning goals.

environment from a child's daily experiences, and thus we encourage practitioners to envision the Environment recommended practices and other topic areas supporting and complementing each other. For example, it is difficult to discuss interaction, instruction, and family practices without also considering the social environment.

Likewise, the physical environment plays a role whenever we consider instruction or transitional practices. Further, the Leadership recommended practices make clear that resources such as space, time, and materials should be available and used by practitioners in their work with children and families. These examples are by no means comprehensive of the multitude of ways the recommended practices intersect with each other, but hopefully they illustrate the rationale behind designating environmental practices as both unique and complementary to all recommended practices.

(2) Environments are fundamental sources of access and participation. Access and participation are the focus of several Environment recommended practices. Access means providing a wide range of activities and opportunities for every child by removing physical barriers, making adaptations, and offering multiple ways to promote engagement for learning and development (DEC/NAEYC, 2009). It can include creating physical space that allows a child who uses a mobility device to move freely or materials to help a child identify pictures as a way to communicate. Access is also embedded in inclusive environments,

where attitudes and beliefs about how and what children with disabilities might be capable of influence their access to learning opportunities.

The International Classification of Functioning and Health model (ICF) by the World Health Organization (WHO) is a framework that describes how individuals with disabilities, including young children, function (World Health Organization, 2001). The ICF defines participation as being involved in life situations and activities. For children this means being part of regular activities and routines in natural environments, that is, any setting where children spend time. According to the ICF, environment is a contextual factor essential to understanding what a child "does do" (their performance) during naturally occurring activities and routines compared with what the same child "can do" (their capacity) under optimal environmental conditions. Enhancing the capacity of an environment therefore influences the capacity of the child so that participation improves and ensures the child is an integral member of a group engaged in certain activities or routines.

(3) Changes to the environment are done in collaboration with the team, including the family, and start from a strengths-based perspective. The Environment recommended practices are purposely broad so that modifications and adaptations to the environment are both universal, so that all children have access, and individualized, so that practitioners consider unique contextual factors for any individual child or family. As practitioners, it can be tempting to identify nonoptimal factors of a specific environment as we decide how, when, and where to suggest changes. However, if our goal is to build the capacity of the environment as a means to increase children's participation, we must start by focusing on strengths when seeking buy-in from the team and family by embodying characteristics of effective coaching (Rush & Shelden, 2011). For example, in the following vignette the practitioner creates an opportunity for dialogue to learn more about a family's strengths, perspectives, and ideas before making suggestions or changes to the environment.

Liz, a developmental therapist, has been visiting Ayeesha and her family for about two months. Ayeesha and her family, refugees from Sudan, live in a small apartment that is part of a resettlement community for refugees from all over the world. During her visits, Liz has observed many caring interactions between Ayeesha and her mother, Samar. However, Liz feels that there is a lack of toys or materials in the apartment for Ayeesha to engage with to increase her social and communication skills. Before taking action to modify Ayeesha's home environment to increase her access to toys and materials, Liz asks Samar questions to learn more about the family and to understand why there may be an absence of toys/materials before proceeding further.

Questions About the Environment Recommended Practices

In the process of identifying guidelines for the recommended practices revisions, the Recommended Practices Commission decided how the practices would be organized. Given the interconnected nature of the Environment recommended practices, certain practices yielded much discussion about which topic areas they should be placed in (e.g., E4, E5, and E6). Given this discussion, we offer answers to two of the most commonly asked questions during presentations of the revised recommended practices.

Why is assistive technology part of the Environment Recommended Practices? Assistive technology (AT) is a broad term describing "any item, piece of equipment, or product system, whether acquired commercially off the shelf, modified, or customized, that is used to increase, maintain, or improve functional capabilities of a child with a disability" (Individuals with Disabilities Education Act, 2004). As such, AT is considered part of the child's physical environment and therefore included under the Environment recommended practices. Practitioners, along with the family and other adults, must identify when a child might benefit from AT and consider other environmental factors, such as the physical space where the AT will be used, the beliefs and values of the family, and how and when AT will be used. Environmental factors across settings, schedules, and caregivers can help or hinder a child's participation, so the practitioner must take all information into consideration before recommending AT and include the family and other adults throughout the assessment and training process.

Why is fitness and wellness included in the Environment Recommended Practices? Regular physical activity is essential for health and development of all children and was intentionally included as an Environment recommended practice because children with or at risk for disabilities and their families face more barriers than those without disabilities for inclusion in formal and informal health and wellness activities (Rimmer & Rowland, 2008). Barriers range from lack of accessible space to cultural beliefs that prohibit children with disabilities from engaging in daily bursts of active play at intensities needed to build strong bodies. The Centers for Disease Control and Prevention (2015) recommends 60 minutes per day of physical activity for children older than age 5. There are no specific recommendations for activity duration for children younger than age 5; however, young children should engage in daily activity during age-appropriate play. Young children with disabilities are not excluded from these recommendations but may have special health care needs requiring medical clearance and supervision. An area that requires more investigation is developing strategies for young children with physical impairments to engage in enough physical activity to improve their overall health and fitness. Practitioners are encouraged to gather information and support families as they discover strategies for safe and regular play that incorporates movement and exploration for children with disabilities, as described in the following vignette.

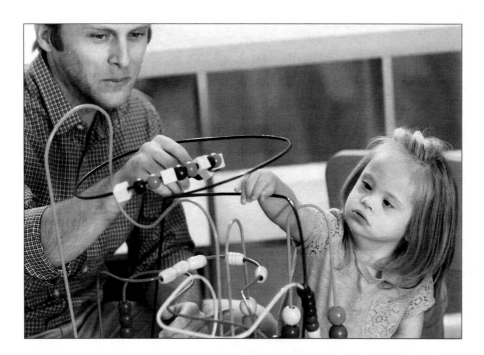

Tammie, an early childhood special education teacher, has always incorporated daily physical activity into her classroom schedule but is feeling concerned about how to do this with her student Benny because of his congenital heart condition. Benny is 5 years old and has had several heart surgeries, the most recent just

one month ago. His parents are supportive but understandably are worried that he could over-exert himself at school. Tammie wants to include Benny in all the classroom activities, but she needs more information to know if and when Benny might need a break. Tammie consults with Benny's parents, the school nurse, and his therapists to gather information and develop a plan so he is included in the regular physical activities but also is monitored for his health and safety. Tammie finds out that children with Benny's condition are usually good at gauging their abilities but that he should not play outside when it is too hot or humid. The nurse writes up some signs to watch out for, and the therapists arranged their schedules so that one of them will be in the classroom or on the playground to help when the children engage in rigorous physical activity.

According to the Healthy People 2020 (U.S. Department of Health and Human Services, n.d.), social and physical environments are determinants of health and can especially contribute to poor health outcomes for people with disabilities. For children with or at risk for disabilities, the cumulative effects of inactivity over a lifetime have long-term consequences. Obesity, hypertension, and diabetes are just a few examples of secondary conditions seen in children with disabilities at higher rates than children without disabilities (Child and Adolescent Health Measurement Initiative, n.d.). Further, adults with disabilities that began in early childhood are at greater risk for myriad other conditions such as osteoporosis, cardiovascular disease, bed sores, and various musculoskeletal injuries, to name a few (Centers for Disease Control and Prevention, 2014).

Finally, infants born with impairments that limit early movement and exploration may miss out on the natural early learning opportunities generally afforded to infants without mobility impairments. Self-initiated movement is linked to cognition, communication, spatial awareness, discrimination of emotion and fear, postural control, perceptual-motor development, visual-motor integration, and problem-solving (Bertenthal & Campos, 1984; Bertenthal & Campos, 1987; Bertenthal, Campos, & Kermoian, 1994; Bushnell & Boudreau, 1993; Herbert, Gross, & Hayne, 2007; Kermoian & Campos, 1988; McEwan, Dihoff, & Brosvic, 1991). Self-initiated movement is a powerful motivator. Infants who can influence their environment are more likely to participate and engage in activities and routines, further developing skills beyond just movement.

Conclusion

Practitioners of early childhood intervention have a responsibility to work alongside families and other adults to provide services in natural and inclusive environments while also influencing features of the environments in ways that will improve child and family outcomes. Overall, the Environment recommended practices promote the access and participation of young children with or at risk for developmental delays or disabilities in everyday learning experiences and naturally occurring routines. We hope that by dedicating Environment as a distinct and essential topic area, practitioners, families, and other stakeholders will work together to enhance the capacity of all environments, thus giving young children with or at risk for developmental delays or disabilities the best chance

> The Environment recommended practices promote the access and participation of young children with or at risk for developmental delays or disabilities in everyday learning experiences and naturally occurring routines.

to participate in the activities they choose and need to grow and develop into healthy, happy, and productive members of their communities and society as a whole.

References

Bertenthal, B. I., & Campos, J. J. (1984). A reexamination of fear and its determinants on the visual cliff. *Psychophysiology, 21,* 413–417. doi:10.1111/j.1469-8986.1984.tb00218.x

Bertenthal, B. I., & Campos, J. J. (1987). New directions in the study of early experience. *Child Development, 58,* 560–567.

Bertenthal, B. I., Campos, J. J., & Kermoian, R. (1994). An epigenetic perspective on the development of self-produced locomotion and its consequences. *Current Directions in Psychological Science, 3,* 140–145.

Bronfenbrenner, U. (1979). *The ecology of human development: Experiments by nature and design.* Cambridge, MA: Harvard University Press.

Bruder, M. B. (2000). Family-centered early intervention: Clarifying our values for the new millennium. *Topics in Early Childhood Special Education, 20,* 105–115. doi:10.1177/027112140002000206

Bushnell, E. W., & Boudreau, J. P. (1993). Motor development and the mind: The potential role of motor abilities as a determinant of aspects of perceptual development. *Child Development, 64,* 1005–1021.

Campbell, P. H., & Milbourne, S. A. (2014). Together is better: Environmental teaching practices to support all children's learning. In K. Pretti-Frontczak, L. Sullivan, & J. Grisham-Brown (Eds.), *YEC monograph series No. 16: Blending practices for all children* (pp. 21–38). Los Angeles, CA: Division for Early Childhood.

Centers for Disease Control and Prevention. (2014, March 31). *Related conditions.* Retrieved from http://www.cdc.gov/ncbddd/disabilityandhealth/relatedconditions.html

Centers for Disease Control and Prevention. (2015, February 11). *How much physical activity do children need?* Retrieved from http://www.cdc.gov/physicalactivity/everyone/guidelines/children.html

Child and Adolescent Health Measurement Initiative. (n.d.). *Data resource center on child and adolescent health.* Retrieved from http://www.childhealthdata.org/

Copple, C., & Bredekamp, S. (Eds.). (2009). *Developmentally appropriate practice in early childhood programs serving children from birth through age 8* (3rd ed.). Washington, DC: National Association for the Education of Young Children.

DEC/NAEYC. (2009). *Early childhood inclusion: A joint position statement of the Division for Early Childhood (DEC) and the National Association for the Education of Young Children (NAEYC).* Chapel Hill: The University of North Carolina, FPG Child Development Institute. Retrieved from http://npdci.fpg.unc.edu/resources/articles/Early_Childhood_Inclusion

Division for Early Childhood. (2014). *DEC recommended practices in early intervention/early childhood special education 2014*. Retrieved from http://www.dec-sped.org/recommendedpractices

Dunst, C. J., Bruder, M. B., Trivette, C. M., Hamby, D., Raab, M., & McLean, M. (2001). Characteristics and consequences of everyday natural learning opportunities. *Topics in Early Childhood Special Education, 21*, 68–92. doi:10.1177/027112140102100202

Herbert, J., Gross, J., & Hayne, H. (2007). Crawling is associated with more flexible memory retrieval by 9-month-old infants. *Developmental Science, 10*, 183–189. doi:10.1111/j.1467-7687.2007.00548.x

Individuals with Disabilities Education Act, 20 U.S.C. § 1400 (2004).

Kermoian, R., & Campos, J. J. (1988). Locomotor experience: A facilitator of spatial cognitive development. *Child Development, 59*, 908–917.

Kolobe, T. H., Arevalo, A., & Catalino, T. A. (2012). The environment of intervention. In S. K. Campbell, R. J. Palisano, & M. N. Orlin (Eds.), *Physical therapy for children* (4th ed., pp. 879–902). St. Louis, MO: Elsevier.

McEwan, M. H., Dihoff, R. E., & Brosvic, G. M. (1991). Early infant crawling experiences is reflected in later motor skill development. *Perceptual and Motor Skills, 72*, 75–79. doi:10.2466/pms.1991.72.1.75

Odom, S. L. (Ed.). (2002). *Widening the circle: Including children with disabilities in preschool programs*. New York, NY: Teachers College Press.

Rimmer, J. H., & Rowland, J. L. (2008). Health promotion for people with disabilities: Implications for empowering the person and promoting disability-friendly environments. *American Journal of Lifestyle Medicine, 2*, 409–420. doi:10.1177/1559827608317397

Rush, D. D., & Shelden, M. L. (2011). *The early childhood coaching handbook*. Baltimore, MD: Paul H. Brookes.

Sandall, S. Hemmeter, M. L., Smith, B. J., & McLean, M. E. (Eds.). (2005). *DEC recommended practices: A comprehensive guide for practical application in early intervention/early childhood special education*. Longmont, CO: Sopris West.

U.S. Department of Health and Human Services. (n.d.). *Determinants of health*. Retrieved from http://www.healthypeople.gov/2020/about/foundation-health-measures/Determinants-of-Health

World Health Organization. (2001). *International classification of functioning, disability and health (ICF)*. Geneva, Switzerland: Author.

6

FAMILY

Using the Recommended Practices to Build Parent Competence and Confidence

CAROL M. TRIVETTE
East Tennessee State University

RASHIDA BANERJEE
University of Northern Colorado

Mr. and Mrs. Gómez have been concerned about their only child Lisa's behavior for the last six months. Lisa's frequent explosive crying and hitting episodes when she's frustrated concerned them, but they thought perhaps it was just "normal" 2-year-old behavior. Two weeks ago, they threw a party to celebrate Lisa's second birthday, inviting family, friends, and neighbors. However, instead of entertaining their guests, Mr. and Mrs. Gómez spent most of the time trying to keep Lisa out of trouble. They were frustrated and embarrassed as Lisa made a fuss and ran around screaming and hitting other children for no apparent reason. This experience clearly showed them that her behavior was not normal. They knew they had to find help. They decided to speak with Mrs. Turner, a social worker they had met through a mutual friend. They were not aware that she was a service coordinator with the local Part C program.

Tim scanned his preschool classroom. Fourteen 3- and 4-year olds were engaged in various activities around the different centers. The paraprofessional and the parent volunteer were working in small groups at the table and in the reading corner. Tim glanced at 4-year-old Mark, who had recently joined his class. Mark was friendly and immediately got along well with his peers, but he seemed to struggle in some areas. On reading his file, Tim had learned that Mark had received a diagnosis of developmental delay and was receiving special education services. Tim had sent out a welcome letter to his parents, Ms. Bower and Ms. Frazier. He had not received a response, and his calls had also remained unanswered. Tim decided to give them a few more days before calling again. In a way he was glad to prolong this meeting. He had not interacted with two parents of the same sex before. He was feeling a little uncomfortable and unsure of his reactions.

Introduction

Given the importance of family participation in a child's development and learning and later success in school and community, one of the seven topics of the revised Division for Early Childhood (DEC) Recommended Practices (2014) emphasizes family practices. The purpose of this article is to provide an overview of these practices, the evidence that supports them, and illustrations that portray how they are used. We further suggest strategies for practitioners to implement the Family recommended practices effectively in their work. Specifically, we answer the following three questions early childhood practitioners frequently ask: What are family practices? Why do practitioners need to implement family practices? How can practitioners implement family practices?

The full list of the DEC Recommended Practices can be found at http://www.dec-sped.org/recommendedpractices. Each practice in the DEC Recommended Practices has a letter and number code. For the Family practices, the letter code is F (F1, F2, etc.). Specific Family recommended practices described here will be referenced using that system.

It is important to define two terms frequently used in this article: *family* and *practice*. We define *family* as "two or more people who regard themselves as a family and who perform some of the functions families typically perform" (A. Turnbull et al., 2010, p. 28). When talking about the adult or adults in the family who work directly with the practitioner to support the child, the term *parent* or *parents* will be used; it is understood that the person might not be the biological or adoptive parent of the child. The term *practitioner* is used to include "those who are responsible for and paid to enhance the optimal development of the child" and promote the knowledge and skills of the parents (Division for Early Childhood, 2014). Practitioners can include, but are not be limited to, early intervention educators, teachers, therapists, child care providers, and social workers. For this section, the term *practices* is defined as methods used to promote parents' gaining the knowledge and skills to support their child's growth and development ("WWC Evidence Review Protocol," n.d.)

What Are Family Practices?

The Family recommended practices guide practitioners' interactions with the parents so practitioners can support parents to participate fully in all decision-making activities regarding their child and to support the development of parents' sense of competence and confidence in helping their child learn and grow. These 10 practices, when used during assessment, planning, and intervention, will ensure that parents have the opportunity to be active participants in all aspects of their child's services. These practices help practitioners interact with families in a manner that conveys to the family the practitioner's belief in the importance of parents' knowledge of and expertise with their child in planning and conducting each aspect of their child's services. The family practices reflect the following underlying principles:

Principle 1: Parents are the constant in the lives of young children with disabilities or at-risk for disabilities and thus are the primary unit of

> "These practices help practitioners interact with families in a manner that conveys to the family the practitioner's belief in the importance of parents' knowledge of and expertise with their child in planning and conducting each aspect of their child's services.

family-centered services (Bruder, 2010). It is the child's parents who move through each transition from hospital to home, home to infant-toddler services, infant-toddler services to preschool services, and preschool services to school-aged services. Though that seems like a lot of transitions, in fact, within each of these contexts frequently several transitions occur as a child moves from one hospital to the next, from one type of therapy to another type of therapy, or from one child care program to another child care program. Because parents are the constant in their child's life, practitioners must recognize how much information parents have and/or may need to have about their child.

Principle 2: Promoting confidence and affirming the competency of the parents to support their child's development and learning is essential in every parent-professional interaction. Because the parent is the constant in the child's life, it is essential that practitioners must consistently focus on helping the families to grow their knowledge, skills, and self-confidence. The more competent (having knowledge and skills) and confident (feeling able to use their knowledge and skills) parents are, the more likely they will continue to provide their children with what they need (Dunst & Trivette, 2009).

Principle 3: The unique characteristics of the family, including but not limited to ethnicity, culture, family structure, and the family's goals, must be respected. Each family's situation is different. Practitioners need to respect the unique characteristics of each family because these characteristics impact how the family wants to support their child and what goals they set for their child.

These three principles can be found in the three themes of the Family recommended practices: family-centered practices, parent capacity-building practices, and parents and professional partnerships/collaborations (Division for Early Childhood, 2014). Family-centered practices are built on a set of values that clearly demonstrate a high regard for each family and emphasize the importance of building trust with the family. The practices are individualized and responsive to specific family situations and the goals for the child. During each interaction with a parent, practitioners must be sensitive to what the parent is trying to communicate and respond in a manner that promotes joint understanding.

Parent capacity-building practices focus on the rightful role of parents as the individuals who are going to provide emotional and physical support to their child for many years to come. It is the obligation of practitioners to support and enhance the parents' capacity to fulfill this role. This is accomplished by providing participatory opportunities and experiences that strengthen existing parental knowledge and skills and promoting the development of new skills when necessary. It is critical that these activities be done in a manner that enhances parents' sense of self-efficacy. The term *self-efficacy* refers to an individual's understanding and acknowledgment of his or her role in accomplishments made (Bandura, 1977). Parents must believe that they are capable of supporting their child's development and learning. This does not mean that parents "do it" alone, but it does mean that practitioners encourage parents to recognize and acknowledge the vital role that the parents themselves play in every accomplishment.

Parents and professionals must work together in a collaborative partnership to accomplish the goals for the child and family. Dunst and Paget (1991) define partnerships between parents and professionals as "an association between a family and one or more professionals who function collaboratively using an agreed-upon role in pursuit of a joint interest and common goal" (p. 29). Using family-centered and parent-capacity building practices is critical when working collaboratively to achieve the goals and outcomes that parents want for their families and their child.

How Strong Is the Research Evidence Behind the Family Recommended Practices?

It is fortunate that there have been many studies that have examined the individual practices that make up the Family recommended practices. Therefore, the evidence for most of these practices is strong. The research evidence for these

practices comes from a number of research articles published in well-established journals in the field. Most of the research evidence for these practices comes from articles that have used either a literature review or meta-analytic review procedure. These two procedures examine many individual research studies to find the similarities or differences in the findings across all studies. The evidence found using these procedures is much stronger than the evidence of any one study.

The logic behind a systematic literature review or meta-analytic review is that any individual research study has the potential of bias that could produce inaccurate study results. Though researchers work to eliminate biases, it is can be difficult to do. Although the finding may be important, a single study reporting that an intervention has a positive effect on a child must be considered with some skepticism because there might be a bias in the study that is not obvious. However, when an intervention has the same positive effect on families or children across many individual studies, skepticism about the accuracy of the finding decreases. R. B. Burns and R. A. Burns (2008) use the analogy of a rope. Each strand of the rope is strong, but when each strand is woven together with other strands, the rope is stronger than a single strand. When the same result is found repeatedly in different studies, it heightens our confidence that the effect is real.

Systemic literature reviews and meta-analysis reviews use many of the same procedures to identify "all" the studies that are related to an intervention practice. After identifying the individual studies, the approaches use different strategies. The researcher doing a systematic review examines and interprets the findings from each study and then develops a balanced and impartial summary of the evidence from all the studies (Uman, 2011). The researcher doing a meta-analysis recodes the data from each individual study to statistically compare the results across all the individual studies (R. B. Burns & R. A. Burns, 2008).

Summary of Research for Individual Family Recommended Practices

The research evidence for 6 of the 10 family practices comes from both a systematic literature review and a meta-analytic review (Dunst & Trivette, 2009; Dunst, Trivette, & Hamby, 2007; Hogan, Linden, & Najarian, 2002; S. King, Teplicky, G. King, & Rosenbaum, 2004; Kuhlthau, et al., 2011; McConachie & Diggle, 2007; Nievar, Van Egeren, & Pollard, 2010; Trivette, Dunst, & Hamby, 2010). The practices that include *both* types of evidence are building trusting and respectful partnerships (F1); providing up-to-date, comprehensive, and unbiased information that families can understand to make decisions (F2); being responsive to family's concerns and changing situations (F3); building family confidence and competence by building family strengths (F5); strengthening family skills and confidence by being flexible (F6); and helping families find formal and informal resources to achieve their goals (F7). Systematic literature review is part of the research evidence for the family practices that focus on practitioners and families working together to accomplish goals (F4).

Clearly there is strong evidence for many of the practices that are included in the Family section of the DEC Recommended Practices. For practitioners, this means that when they use these practices as described, the results are likely to be that parents feel more competent and confident in their abilities to support their child.

Why Do We Need to Implement the Family Recommended Practices?

The major reason that we want to implement Family recommended practices when working with families is the same reason we want to implement evidence-based practices in our work with children. We want children to reach their highest potential and be able to live full and rewarding lives. We want to build the capacity of the parents to support their child's learning at home and to get the resources and services that are important to promote their child's growth and development. In short, we want the very *best* outcomes for children not only while we are working with them as young children, but we want positive outcomes for them in the years to come, long after we are no longer in their lives. Because we are only in the lives of these children and parents for a short

> Using family-centered and parent-capacity building practices is critical when working collaboratively to achieve the goals and outcomes that parents want for their families and their child.

period of time, it is imperative that we use every interaction with a parent as an opportunity to boost their knowledge, skills, and confidence for acquiring what their child needs to reach their full potential. Specifically we want parents to have knowledge about and an understanding of their child's strengths and condition, various types of formal (services) and informal resources and supports available to their child and them, and their child's and family's legal rights. In each of these three areas, we want parents to feel competent in their knowledge and understanding and believe in *their abilities* to achieve what they want and need for their child.

The use of the Family recommended practices can also have positive outcomes for practitioners. When practitioners use these practices with accuracy and precision (fidelity) while working with a family, they can be confident that the parents will grow in their competence and confidence. Practitioners will see families being able to support their child in new ways. The practitioner working with the family in this manner will be more likely to see progress in the child's growth and development.

> We want parents to have knowledge about and an understanding of their child's strengths and condition, various types of formal (services) and informal resources and supports available to their child and them, and their child's and family's legal rights.

How Can Practitioners Implement the Family Recommended Practices?

Children develop and learn within the context of their families and cultures (Barton & Banerjee, 2013; Lynch & Hanson, 2011). Children need to learn the skills and behaviors that ensure acceptance, participation, and membership in their families and communities. Thus, it is critical that practitioners provide services that promote active participation of families in decision-making related to their child that leads to the development of a service plan and that support families in achieving the goals they hold for their child and other family members (Division for Early Childhood, 2014). Returning to the examples presented earlier, we illustrate Family recommended practices in home-based and center-based settings through the interactions between Mrs. Turner and the Gómez family and Tim and Mark's parents.

How Do Practitioners Introduce These Practices to Families in a Home-based Setting?

Mrs. Turner scheduled a meeting with Mr. and Mrs. Gómez at their home on a mutually convenient day in the evening so both parents could be present (F3). Knowing that English was not their home language, she also offered to bring an interpreter and a cultural broker if needed by the family (F1). However, feeling confident that they could convey their concerns relatively well in English, the family declined this offer. Mrs. Turner also sought their permission to bring a colleague with her who was better equipped to answer their questions about Lisa's development.

Before the start of the meeting, Mrs. Turner greeted the family and introduced her colleague, Ms. Romm, a developmental interventionist (F1). Mrs. Turner explained to the family about the process her agency used to determine whether Lisa might need services and their rights and responsibilities. She provided them with a written copy of the information in Spanish (F9). During the meeting, Mrs.

Turner asked the family about their typical day. Using open-ended questions, she also inquired about other routines, what was working, and challenges or concerns they had with Lisa's development (F3). Ms. Romm observed the interactions, asked probing questions, and took notes. She also asked Mr. and Mrs. Gómez if they would be willing to serve as play facilitators during a formal assessment to help the evaluation team answer specific questions by engaging Lisa in both familiar play routines and new play activities in her home language (F6).

At the end of the meeting, Ms. Romm reviewed the information they had gathered with Mr. and Mrs. Gómez in jargon-free language, with the help of drawings and charts (F2). She described Lisa's strengths and possible areas of need. Ms. Romm asked the Gómezes whether they had any questions. Mr. Gómez asked whether they should speak with Lisa only in English because he had heard that children are confused by two languages. Ms. Romm assured the family that this was a myth that is not supported by research. She also described language development in bilingual children with and without disabilities in simple, easy-to-understand language (F2, F8).

Before leaving, Ms. Romm provided the family with a couple of initial strategies to work on at home and in other natural environments during their routines to prevent Lisa's behavior challenges during the day (F5). For example, during the morning when Lisa fusses before brushing her teeth, Ms. Romm suggested turning on her favorite song so that she could listen while she is brushing. Explaining that offering children choices is a powerful strategy to prevent challenging behavior, Ms. Romm suggested that they keep two toothbrushes so Lisa could choose which toothbrush to use each morning (F6). Ms. Romm also made a note to share information about accessible parent education and training activities at their next meeting (F6).

How Do Practitioners Introduce These Practices to Families in a Center-based Setting?

When Tim called Mark's home again during his lunch break, a woman's voice answered. Tim introduced himself. Ms. Frazier immediately apologized for not responding to his earlier calls; she and Ms. Bower had to deal with a family emergency. She said they would like to drop by the preschool to say hello to Mark's new teacher in person and see how Mark was doing in the classroom. They set a time to meet at school on the following Tuesday afternoon when Ms. Bower could get away from work and when Tim could find another adult to supervise outdoor time with the children (F3).

Tim waited anxiously on the day of the meeting. When the receptionist announced Ms. Bower and Ms. Frazier's arrival, he went out to greet them (F1). He formally shook hands with them and led them to a quiet room where they could watch Mark playing outdoors as they talked. He could not help but notice that the two women appeared relaxed and watched their son play outside with pleasure. He found his anxiety receded as he realized that this couple were parents who loved their son deeply.

Tim explained the program and its goals, philosophy, and vision. He also shared a copy of the program's welcome letter and some literature about the program that informed the parents about their rights (F2, F9). When Ms. Frazier asked how Mark was doing in the preschool, Tim shared how friendly he was with other children. Mark had even helped out last week with the snack table. Ms. Bower and Ms. Frazier smiled and exchanged glances knowingly; Mark loved to help and he would take every opportunity possible to help in the house! His doing the same at school reassured them that he was comfortable enough to be himself in this new environment. Tim then shared the reports that he had printed out from the initial assessment that he had completed on Mark. He highlighted Mark's strengths in social-emotional skills and in communication with peers and adults. However, using examples, Tim explained that Mark was not performing as well in early literacy and conceptual learning (F2). Tim listened as Ms. Bower acknowledged that she also had been concerned that when she read books to him (F3, F5), Mark would not remember the front of a book or

incidents in a book that he had heard multiple times. Similarly, he had a hard time completing familiar puzzles.

Tim then shared information on the goals they were already working on and wondered whether the parents had any other suggestions (F4). Tim agreed to try the parents' suggestions to help Mark concentrate in school (F5). At Ms. Bower's request, he also promised to send them links for audiovisual resources on how to read with children. Because Mark and his family were new to the town, Tim shared some community resources (F7). Finally, when Ms. Frazier asked if there was anything else they could do, Tim took this opportunity to let them know about family volunteering and other opportunities in which they could participate (F10).

Just as Mark's parents were leaving, the children returned from outdoors. Tim said goodbye and left for his class. He felt relieved and pleased at how the meeting had gone. He also noticed a tinge of embarrassment at his prior dread and discomfort. He made a mental note to be aware of making judgments henceforth.

Conclusion

In both of the previous examples, practitioners worked with families in a manner that enhanced the families' competence and confidence. Clearly the Family recommended practices were part of the practice repertoire of the practitioners in these scenarios. However, it can be challenging for practitioners to sustain these practices over time with diverse families. Practitioners need to be supported to learn and sustain their use of all DEC Recommended Practices, but especially the Family practices. All families are unique and their circumstances, concerns, strengths, and dreams combine to make their distinctive situations. Often practitioners who are comfortable using these practices with one family find that when they are working with another family, the strategies that worked previously no longer seem to be effective. In these situations, practitioners need support and guidance about how to explore and reflect on their interactions with the family to determine what changes could be made to their current practices and what new strategies they might try.

This support can be found in a variety of ways; some may currently exist while others might need to be created. A supervisor or team member can be a resource for finding this type of support. In some agencies, practitioners have developed learning communities, some of which are focused on specific areas while others are focused on a variety of topics. DEC has two groups of practitioner members that focus on supporting each other when using DEC Recommended Practices through special interest groups (SIG): the Early Intervention SIG and the Inclusion SIG. (Information about these groups can be found at http://www.dec-sped.org/sigs) Additional resources for implementing Family recommended practices are provided in the Resources Within Reason article in this monograph. The definition of terms used in the Family recommended practices and additional examples for each of the Family recommended practices can be found at http://www.dec-sped.org/recommendedpractices.

The Family recommended practices in the 2014 DEC's Recommended Practices provide guidance to practitioners in using evidence-based practices that build trusting relationships with families, treat families with dignity and respect, strengthen families' confidence and knowledge, and ensure the active involvement of family members in all decision-making processes to improve child and family outcomes (Trivette et al., 2010). Implementation of Family recommended practices involves an ongoing process of self-reflection and growth so practitioners can engage in a continuing awareness of their values, beliefs, biases, and assumptions and make sure these do not impact their work with families.

References

Bandura, A. (1977). Self-efficacy: Toward a unifying theory of behavioral change. *Psychological Review, 84*, 191–215. doi:10.1037/0033-295X.84.2.191

Barton, E. E., & Banerjee, R. (2013). Culturally responsive behavioral supports for children with challenging behaviors and their families. In M. M. Ostrosky & S. Sandall (Eds.), *YEC monograph series No. 15: Addressing young children's challenging behaviors* (pp. 76–94). Missoula, MT: Division for Early Childhood.

Bruder, M. B. (2010). Early childhood intervention: A promise to children and families for their future. *Exceptional Children, 76,* 339–355. doi:10.1177/001440291007600306

Burns, R. B., & Burns, R. A. (2008). *Business research methods and statistics using SPSS.* Thousand Oaks, CA: Sage

Division for Early Childhood. (2014). *DEC recommended practices in early intervention/early childhood special education 2014.* Retrieved from http://www.dec-sped.org/recommendedpractices

Dunst, C. J., & Paget, K. D. (1991). Parent-professional partnerships and family empowerment. In M. J. Fine (Ed.), *Collaboration with parents of exceptional children* (pp. 25–44). Brandon, VT: Clinical Psychology.

Dunst, C. J., & Trivette, C. M. (2009). Meta-analytic structural equation modeling of the influences of family-centered care on parent and child psychological health. *International Journal of Pediatrics, 2009,* 1–9. doi:10.1155/2009/576840

Dunst, C. J., Trivette, C. M., & Hamby, D. W. (2007). Meta-analysis of family-centered helpgiving practices research. *Mental Retardation and Developmental Disabilities Research Reviews, 13,* 370–378. doi:10.1002/mrdd.20176

Hogan, B. E., Linden, W., & Najarian, B. (2002). Social support interventions: Do they work? *Clinical Psychology Review, 22,* 381–440. doi:10.1016/S0272-7358(01)00102-7

King, S., Teplicky, R., King, G., & Rosenbaum, P. (2004). Family-centered service for children with cerebral palsy and their families: A review of the literature. *Seminars in Pediatric Neurology, 11,* 78–86. doi:10.1016/j.spen.2004.01.009

Kuhlthau, K. A., Bloom, S., Van Cleave, J., Knapp, A. A., Romm, D., Klatka, K., . . . Perrin, J. M. (2011). Evidence for family-centered care for children with special health care needs: A systematic review. *Academic Pediatrics, 11,* 136–143. doi:10.1016/j.acap.2010.12.014

Lynch, E. W., & Hanson, M. J. (Eds.). (2011). *Developing cross-cultural competence: A guide for working with children and their families* (4th ed.). Baltimore, MD: Paul H. Brookes.

McConachie, H., & Diggle, T. (2007). Parent implemented early intervention for young children with autism spectrum disorder: A systematic review. *Journal of Evaluation in Clinical Practice, 13,* 102–129. doi:10.1111/j.1365-2753.2006.00674.x

Nievar, M. A., Van Egeren, L. A., & Pollard, S. (2010). A meta-analysis of home visiting programs: Moderators of improvements in maternal behavior. *Infant Mental Health Journal, 31,* 499–520. doi:10.1002/imhj.20269

Trivette, C. M., Dunst, C. J., & Hamby, D. W. (2010). Influences of family-systems intervention practices on parent-child interactions and child development. *Topics in Early Childhood Special Education, 30,* 3–19. doi:10.1177/0271121410364250

Turnbull, A., Turnbull, R., Erwin, E., Soodak, L., & Shogren, K. (2010). *Families, professionals, and exceptionality: Positive outcomes through partnerships and trust* (6th ed.). Upper Saddle River, NJ: Pearson.

Uman, L. S. (2011). Systematic reviews and meta-analyses. *Journal of the Canadian Academy of Child and Adolescent Psychiatry, 20*, 57–59. Retrieved from http://www.cacap-acpea.org/

WWC evidence review protocol for early childhood education interventions for children with disabilities, version 2.0. (n.d.). Washington, DC: Institute of Education Sciences. Retrieved from http://ies.ed.gov/ncee/wwc/document.aspx?sid=30

7

INSTRUCTION

Making the Most of Learning Opportunities

ILENE SCHWARTZ
University of Washington

JULIANN WOODS
Florida State University

CHILDREN LEARN BY DOING. THEY LEARN BY INTERACTING WITH their social and physical environment, observing, and practicing skills and behaviors that enable them to be successful, competent, and self-directed learners. Instruction, the intentional arrangement of the environment to enhance learning, plays an active and essential role. It is one of the strategies that adults can use to help children learn important, functional skills and behaviors. Those are the skills and behaviors that are going to help improve the lives of children with disabilities or who are at risk for disabilities and their families. Instruction includes planning, environment arrangement (e.g., arranging materials, the role of adults, the role of peers), opportunities to practice, and systematic feedback.

The purpose of instructional practices is to help children acquire the skills and behaviors that will help them be more independent and successful as young children and throughout their lives. That means that the instructional practices used in early intervention/early childhood special education programs must address all four phases of the learning process. These phases are:

- Acquisition—learning how to do the skill.
- Fluency—learning to do the skill smoothly and at natural rates.
- Maintenance—learning to do the skill after instruction has stopped.
- Generalization—learning to apply the skill whenever and wherever it is needed and not to apply the skill when it is unnecessary or inappropriate (e.g., talking loudly while inside or standing up when the teacher is reading a story; Wolery, Bailey, & Sugai, 1988).

Common Characteristics of Instructional Strategies

Although there are many variables on which instructional strategies vary, such as theoretical perspective, there are some characteristics that are common to all recommended instructional strategies:

- They are intentional.
- They use data-based decision making.
- They address goals and objectives across disciplines.
- They are individualized.
- They build on strengths, preferences, and interests.
- They align with family beliefs and values.

Instructional practices that address all four stages of learning enable parents, interventionists, and other caregivers to help children learn skills that will be durable, can be used across all environments (e.g., home, school, community), and will ultimately improve the quality of life for children and their families.

Instructional practices include a diverse group of strategies that range from those that are child initiated (e.g., incidental teaching) to those that are adult initiated (e.g., discrete trial teaching). Some instructional practices fit well in the natural environments in which young children spend most of their time (e.g., home, child care, community) and others fit better into more decontextualized teaching sessions that may be provided for children with significant delays or specialized learning needs (e.g., individual speech therapy, physical therapy, or behavioral therapy).

Instructional practices also address how adults interact with each other to intentionally promote child learning and development. Although there are many characteristics that are shared by instructional practices, one of the most important is that the instructional targets they address are selected to meet the needs of individual children and their families and the instructional practices are designed to fit into the lives of those children and families. The following two examples illustrate the application of instructional practices.

Johnie's Story

Brian and Sophia Anderson knew their daughter had spina bifida prior to her delivery. As they prepared for her arrival, they envisioned a delicate daughter who would need extra health care and learning supports. They were anxious but determined to nurture and teach her. She was born with myelomeningocele, the most serious type of spina bifida in which a sac of fluid came through an opening in her back, damaging part of the spinal cord and nerves in this sac. Her surgical repair went well. While the physicians cautioned her parents that future outcomes would depend on the neural damage, the Andersons were confident. They named her Ilyana Grace after her great grandmothers, who were librarians and their families' first college graduates. Not everything continued as Brian and Sophia had anticipated for their baby girl. She had difficulties with breastfeeding and lost weight. Her stay in the neonatal intensive care unit (NICU) was extended after she got an infection following the placement of a shunt.

Melia, an early intervention special instructor, met Brian and Sophia at the NICU and began serving as Ilyana's primary service provider before she came home. As the primary service provider, Melia took the lead working with Brian and Sophia and the rest of the medical and intervention team to plan and implement supports and services during her hospital stay and the transition home. The focus of intervention in the first few weeks at home was on staying healthy, resolving the feeding challenges, and gaining weight. Sleep was also a priority for everyone in the family! Brian and Sophia gained knowledge about spina bifida and its impact on their daughter and their lives from their early intervention (EI) and health care team. They gained confidence in feeding her and monitoring her shunt, and they began to enjoy playing with her.

Next Steps in Early Intervention: Embedded Instruction

At 6 months, Brian and Sophia nicknamed their daughter Johnie and described her as a spitfire, full of noise, impatience, and wonder. They laughed at their belief that she inherited her independent and opinionated nature from her ancestors rather than the quiet demeanor of a librarian. They were surprised by her noisy and energetic interactions with them and were happy her feeding and other health care needs were improving. They recognized the importance of monitoring her weight gain, health, and physical development, but they also believed it was time for her coming out party. Johnie was demanding participation rather than protection. The good news was Melia and the EI team were ready, and at their individualized family support plan (IFSP) review, they introduced the DEC Recommended Practices as a strategy to guide their planning and intervention implementation and to ensure continued coordination with the health care professionals.

Melia initiated the IFSP review with INS1, "Practitioners, with the family, identify each child's strengths, preferences, and interests to engage the child in active learning," as a strategy to update the IFSP outcomes. She asked Brian and Sophia to share what Johnie does that makes them smile. Melia's question focused the team, her parents, the physical therapist, and the speech language pathologist on Johnie's strengths and how to use them to engage her in learning. Sophia started the conversation by sharing all the ways Johnie lets her know she wants to be moved or positioned differently, including squeals, whimpers, yells, and, recently, some arm flapping that looks a bit like she wants to fly. Sophia also shared that Johnie was reaching to grab at her mother's arm and at the dog's tail when they go by! Brian said Johnie loved to be with people, wanted to be in the middle of the action, and sought attention from others, including Max, their dog. Brian and Sophia described her as feisty and believed her interest in people and their activities was a great place to start engaging her active learning.

Melia used this conversation as a jumping off point for the next instructional practice, INS2: "Practitioners, with the family, identify skills to target for instruction that help a child become adaptive, competent, socially connected, and engaged and that promote learning in natural and inclusive environments." Melia saw Brian walk by Johnie sitting in her infant chair on the table during the meeting. He stooped, spoke to her, and touched her face before he continued to the kitchen for a drink. Johnie struggled to look up from her reclined position to find her dad, but he was out of sight. She vocalized and then started to cry. Dad circled back, picked her up while turning to Melia, and said, "This happens more all the time. She yells or cries even though we are right here. We wish she would let us know what she wants without crying. We worry when she cries that she will make herself sick."

To explore Johnie's communication needs, the speech language pathologist asked Brian if there were other times when it would help if Johnie could let them know what she wanted. Brian listed several different times and activities, such as when she gets tired of playing in her chair, when she wants to eat, and when she drops all her toys on the floor and wants them back. Sophia added that Johnie cries when she just gets bored and wants someone to pick her up. Sophia commented that they move her infant seat to the room they are in so Johnie is not alone. She added that because Johnie is more active, they can't put her chair up on the kitchen counter or table for fear she will tip it over. Sophia asked about options for positioning Johnie throughout the day. She wondered about getting her out of her chair for more floor time and sitting up by herself.

With support from the team, Brian and Sophia identified several of Johnie's strengths, including increased interest in social interaction, more intentional vocalizations and motor actions, and additional motivation to participate in activity around her. They described some potential targets, including supported sitting and intentional use of sounds and early gestures, such as lifting her arms to ask to be picked up from her chair or crib and reaching to request an object she dropped on the floor. They also named a few things they do throughout the day, such as mealtime, naps, and playtime on the floor as possible routines and settings to work on helping her learn. These early developing skills have both immediate and long-term functionality for Johnie. They provide immediate usefulness and over time will serve as a foundation for the development of more sophisticated social, communication, and motor skills.

Instruction embedded in naturally occurring activities and routines is a cornerstone of early intervention (Dunst, Hamby, Trivette, Raab, & Bruder, 2000). Research has shown that young children learn in their daily routines and that caregivers are effective at teaching their children during these natural interactions. Learning within everyday routines and activities is efficient and meaningful for both the child and the caregiver. The child is motivated to participate in the activity, engage and interact with familiar caregivers, and acquire the target skill and gain fluency through repeated practice throughout the day. Brian and Sophia identified a minimum of 10 opportunities for Johnie to request to be picked up during the day and at least another 10 to request objects that she wants or enjoys. By problem solving with the physical therapist, they built a pillow chair on the floor that provided support but also promoted strengthening core muscles for independent sitting. Instruction is intentional and systematic; it doesn't just happen. Under this approach, the caregiver deliberately embeds instruction within and across routines and environments to provide contextually relevant learning opportunities for the child (INS5).

Melia's next step was to support Brian and Sophie using a coaching approach that facilitates positive adult-child interactions and instruction designed to promote Johnie's skill development (INS13) during home visits. Coaching engages the EI provider and the parents in a triad with the child where the provider supports the teaching interactions between the parents and their child (Rush & Shelden, 2011; Woods, Wilcox, Friedman, & Murch, 2011). The coach builds on the parents' interactional strengths, observes what is working well, and teaches instructional strategies to the parents to use within the routine and throughout the day.

As each home visit unfolds, Melia, Brian, and Sophia exchange information and experiences on the what, when, where, and how component of embedded intervention, or the specific strategies to use with Johnie during the routines to support her practice and participation. Brian is all about playtime on the floor, so after Melia quickly explained and demonstrated how to attract Johnie's interest while she sat in the newly developed "pillow chair," Brian sat facing Johnie and placed a favorite toy in sight but just out of reach. Johnie looked, and with a little support, she reached for it. Brian asked Melia about which toys were easiest to grasp and tried again. Melia, Brian, and Sophia planned for and provided the level of support, accommodations, and adaptations needed for Johnie to access, participate, and learn within and across activities and routines (INS4.)

Brian and Sophia wanted to understand and expand Johnie's communication. Melia shared evidence that parent-implemented communication interventions have positive, significant outcomes for the development of gestures and expressive language (Kaiser & Roberts, 2013). Together they selected the "how" intervention strategies that worked for both of them: (a) responding to Johnie's communication; (b) expanding on her communication signals; and (c) balancing their communication turns with her to establish reciprocal exchanges. Melia coached them to use these strategies with fidelity (INS6) and to collect data that will allow them to make decisions about Johnie's progress and the program (INS3).

The routines identified by the family provided many opportunities for Brian and Sophia to try and see what works the best for them and for Johnie. Melia coached Brian and Sophia to practice the strategies, and together they problem solved and reflected on which intervention strategies worked for both the child and the caregiver, what might need modification, and when it was time to extend the learning further to new targets or additional contexts (INS4). Coaching provided the opportunities for the team to plan, practice, problem solve, and review so the family's daily routines became the instruction that promoted Johnie's learning and development.

> Research has shown that young children learn in their daily routines and that caregivers are effective at teaching their children during natural interactions. Learning within everyday routines and activities is efficient and meaningful for both the child and the caregiver.

Raymond's Story

Raymond Salazar was a 4-year-old boy with twin sisters who had just started first grade. He loved to be outside running, climbing, and riding bikes. In fact, he started walking early at 9 months and started to run the day after he started to walk. He loved music and letters. One of his favorite things to do was to play with the letter tiles from a board game and create words that he had seen on television, in applications on his tablet, and in books. He did not say any words until he was 20 months old, but his parents and their pediatrician did not worry because they all believed that sometimes boys start talking late, especially with older sisters talking for him. But when he was seen by a new pediatrician for his 2-year-old checkup, she was concerned and suggested the parents have him screened. Raymond was diagnosed with autism spectrum disorder at 28 months and started receiving early intervention immediately. The day after his third birthday, he entered an early childhood special education program offered by his local school district. He attended preschool at his neighborhood school, the same one his sisters attend. The school district adopted the Project DATA model (Schwartz, Sandall, McBride, & Boulware, 2004), so he attended an inclusive preschool five days a week. In addition, three days a week he had an extended day, during which he received intensive instruction. His family also participated in a monthly home visit and monthly parent education and support programs at the school.

The staff of the early childhood special education program (ECSE) that Raymond attended prides itself on using the DEC Recommended Practices to guide their program. One of the strategies that the teachers use to inform parents about the DEC Recommended Practices is to introduce them at the annual preschool curriculum night, provide a copy for every family, and then reference them at the monthly home visit and the annual IEP meetings. Dr. and Mrs. Salazar (Raymond's parents) were active members of Raymond's school team, and they met with the other members of the team prior to beginning to develop his current IEP. The team was led by the special education teacher, who was in charge of the extended day part of his program, and included a multidisciplinary team of professionals, including his preschool teacher, his speech language pathologist, and his occupational therapist. The team reviewed assessment reports and Raymond's strengths and areas of need, and it developed a list of potential goals and objectives. They then prioritized the list, considering which goals were most appropriate to be taught in which contexts and putting together an IEP for Raymond's last year of preschool (INS1).

Raymond spent about half of his time at school in an inclusive preschool classroom (Strain, Schwartz & Barton, 2011). His preschool teacher, special education teacher, speech language pathologist, and occupational therapist developed an activity matrix (Schwartz, Sandall, & Gauvreau, 2013) for the classroom. The purpose of this matrix was to display, on one page, all of Raymond's IEP objectives and when the specially designed instruction for each objective would be implemented during the preschool day (INS 4 & 5). Raymond's teacher designed this form so it could also be used to collect data to ensure the team had child performance data to review at its twice monthly meeting and these data could be used to make decisions about programming (i.e., data-based decision making, INS3).

Raymond's team also used visual supports to help him learn at school, home, and in the community (INS 4). They had found that these visual supports helped Raymond be more independent and use newly acquired skills across different settings (Gauvreau & Schwartz, 2013). Like all instructional practices, the use of visual supports for Raymond was planned very carefully before they were implemented. The team brainstormed about what time of day Raymond needed more support to be actively engaged and then planned visual supports to accomplish this goal (INS6). One of the most successful uses of visual supports for Raymond was an activity schedule to help him sample all of the centers at school and play independently at home. Once this schedule was developed, Raymond was taught how to use it using direct instruction and explicit positive consequences for demonstrating the target behavior (INS7). One positive side effect of teaching Raymond to use the activity schedule was that  once he became proficient with it, teachers were able to greatly reduce the amount of positive reinforcement because Raymond's behavior was now being reinforced by the play activities and interactions with peers on the schedule.

Raymond spent the other half of his day in a classroom where he received explicit, intensive instruction (INS10). During this part of the day, teachers provided instruction in both decontextualized and embedded settings. The instruction conducted in decontextualized settings usually involves discrete trial training of communication and cognitive concepts that Raymond was just beginning to learn. The instruction in embedded settings usually includes use of natural developmental behavioral interventions (e.g., pivotal response treatment) in the classroom and in other locations in the school (Schreibman et al., 2015). All of the instruction was intended to increase Raymond's engagement in the planned classroom activities and to promote meaningful progress toward important educational outcomes (INS6).

Throughout Raymond's instructional day, he interacted with many different teaching staff, including general education teachers, special education teachers, para-professionals, speech language pathologists, occupational therapists, and student teachers. To ensure all members of Raymond's school team implemented the instructional strategies with high fidelity, all staff participated in training at the beginning of the school year and could request shoulder-to-shoulder coaching if they wanted assistance in the classroom. In addition, the special education supervisor for the school district observed in the classroom monthly and provided written feedback to all staff members (INS13).

One behavior that had most concerned Dr. and Mrs. Salazar since Raymond's diagnosis was his aggression. Although they had seen a dramatic

decrease in the frequency of this behavior, they were still worried about its impact on their family, his peers, and the classroom. Shortly after his diagnosis, Raymond's parents noticed that he was hitting them and his sisters when things "didn't seem to go his way." They told the teachers about it, and the teachers stated they had seen a few instances of the behavior at school and scheduled a home visit to observe the behavior.

After the home visit, the team convened to make a plan. It completed a functional behavior assessment and determined the behavior appeared to be motivated by a need for attention (INS9). The team brainstormed ideas about effective and sustainable intervention alternatives that taught Raymond a functionally equivalent and socially appropriate skill (Koegel & Frea, 1993). The team decided to teach Raymond how to ask for help when he needed it and for the attention from an adult when he wanted it. The strategy is called *functional communication training* (Carr & Durand, 1985). Through the combination of teaching an appropriate alternative behavior and ignoring the inappropriate behavior when it occurred, the frequency of this behavior had decreased to about once a week. Raymond's parents and teacher agreed that as his language skills and play improved, his aggression decreased. All the team members agreed that Raymond had more strategies to solve problems when things "don't go his way," so aggression no longer served the function it once did.

Raymond had made a tremendous amount of progress in the two and half years since receiving a diagnosis of ASD. His parents were confident they had acquired the skills to advocate for their son and teach him many of the skills he would need to be successful at home, school, and in the community. His teachers were proud of the work they had done to help Raymond acquire skills across all developmental domains and were confident he was going to be successful in kindergarten and beyond.

Summary and Conclusions

Instructional practices are a cornerstone of early intervention and early childhood special education. They are intentional and systematic strategies to inform what to teach, when to teach, how to evaluate the effects of teaching, and how to support and evaluate the quality of instructional practices implemented by others. As demonstrated by the two case studies above, instructional practices are an important component of early intervention/early childhood special education for children of all ages and all abilities. Although the location of the instruction, the type of interaction contained within the instructional interaction, the people providing the instruction, and the goals of the instruction may vary, there are core components shared by all high-quality instructional practices.

Implementing instructional practices with fidelity embodies early intervention/early childhood special education. Instructional practices are the tools that interventionists and families use to help change the developmental trajectories of children with disabilities. That is, these strategies are the tools of our trade. They enable interventionists around the world to help children such as Johnie and Raymond learn new skills, achieve meaningful outcomes, and participate as full members of their communities.

References

Carr, E. G., & Durand, V. M. (1985). Reducing behavior problems through functional communication training. *Journal of Applied Behavior Analysis, 18,* 111–126. doi:10.1901/jaba.1985.18-111

Dunst, C. J., Hamby, D., Trivette, C. M., Raab, M., & Bruder, M. B. (2000). Everyday family and community life and children's naturally occurring learning opportunities. *Journal of Early Intervention, 23,* 151–164. doi:10.1177/1053815 1000230030501

Gauvreau, A. N., & Schwartz, I. S. (2013). Using visual supports to promote appropriate behavior in young children with autism and related disabilities. In M. M. Ostrosky & S. R. Sandall (Eds.), *YEC monograph series No. 15: Addressing young children's challenging behaviors* (pp. 29–44). Missoula, MT: Division for Early Childhood.

Kaiser, A. P., & Roberts, M. Y. (2013). Parent-implemented enhanced milieu teaching with preschool children who have intellectual disabilities. *Journal of Speech, Language, and Hearing Research, 56,* 295–309. doi:10.1044/1092-4388(2012/11-0231)

Koegel, R. L., & Frea, W. D. (1993). Treatment of social behavior in autism through the modification of pivotal social skills. *Journal of Applied Behavior Analysis, 26,* 369–377. doi:10.1901/jaba.1993.26-369

Core Components Shared by All High-Quality Instructional Practices

High-quality instructional practices:

- are intentional.
- address target skills and behaviors that are priorities for the family.
- address pivotal skills and behaviors that help to make the child more independent.
- use data-based decision making to ensure that the instructional practices are designed to help children make the most progress possible.
- are implemented with high fidelity.

Rush, D. D., & Shelden, M. L. (2011). *The early childhood coaching handbook.* Baltimore, MD: Paul H. Brookes.

Schreibman, L., Dawson, G., Stahmer, A. C., Landa, R., Rogers, S. J., McGee, G. G., ... & Halladay, A. (2015). Naturalistic developmental behavioral interventions: Empirically validated treatments for autism spectrum disorder. *Journal of Autism and Developmental Disorders,* 1–18. doi:10.1007/s10803-015-2407-8

Schwartz, I. S., Sandall, S. R., & Gauvreau, A. N. (2013). Planning to individualize: Meeting the needs of all children using activity matrices. *Teaching Young Children, 7*(2), 21–23.

Schwartz, I. S., Sandall, S. R., McBride, B. J., & Boulware, G.-L. (2004). Project DATA (developmentally appropriate treatment for autism): An inclusive school-based approach to educating young children with autism. *Topics in Early Childhood Special Education, 24,* 156–168.

Strain, P. S., Schwartz, I. S., & Barton, E. E. (2011). Providing interventions for young children with autism spectrum disorders: What we still need to accomplish. *Journal of Early Intervention, 33,* 321–332. doi:10.1177/1053815111429970

Wolery, M., Bailey, D. B., Jr., & Sugai, G. M. (1988). *Effective teaching: Principles and procedures of applied behavior analysis with exceptional students.* Boston, MA: Allyn and Bacon.

Woods, J. J., Wilcox, M. J., Friedman, M., & Murch, T. (2011). Collaborative consultation in natural environments: Strategies to enhance family-centered supports and services. *Language, Speech, and Hearing Services in Schools, 42,* 379–392. doi:10.1044/0161-1461(2011/10-0016)

INTERACTION

From Qualities of Interaction to Intervention Practices: Using What Comes Naturally

JEANETTE MCCOLLUM
University of Illinois at Urbana-Champaign

8

You are looking forward to your next conversation with Gretchen. You've been planning a vacation and are eager to get her ideas and hear more about her new job. You and Gretchen have been friends for a long time and have always enjoyed being together. As you talk, you think about how wonderful it feels to share a good conversation with someone you know so well. As you say good-bye, both of you are already looking forward to the next time you can be together.

As you reflect on your conversation, you think about how different your interactions are with Gretchen than with the young children with whom you work. How is it, though each of you have your individual characteristics and ways of communicating—and certainly don't agree about everything—that you and Gretchen always manage to achieve such an enjoyable interaction? What is it that allows your individual characteristics and ways of communicating to blend into an enjoyable, effortless whole? One thing you might think about is how you share an interest in one another's lives so that as you talk, your conversation revolves around a shared topic of interest. This not only allows each of you to maintain the topic but to extend on it with new thoughts and feelings, creating a partnership in moving the conversation forward. Something else that might occur to you is that during your conversation each of you used not only words but also nonverbal signals such as eye contact, tone of voice, and facial expression to convey your interest, to make your meaning clear, and to indicate that you understood each other's meaning. The two of you took turns talking and listening. Each of you felt comfortable waiting, knowing that your turn would come.

You realize that you and Gretchen have grown to trust one another as conversational partners and that most of this happened naturally. Until now, you never gave it much thought. But now you wonder about how interactions that young children have with adults or with other children develop into the kind of interactions that you have with Gretchen. You begin to envision how the way you and other adults interact with a child might, over time, lead that child toward gradually learning the same kinds of communicative acts and roles that you and Gretchen enjoy with one another. You also see how the quality of interactions over time could become the basis for enduring, mutually enjoyable relationships. You think about your interactions with the young children you know. How are these interactions the same and different from those between adults? Are there characteristics and qualities of interactions that are helpful to children, and those that are not? Does the quality of early interactions contribute to how children develop and learn, and to what they become? Can adults learn to use the characteristics of interaction that help children to become competent, confident interactors as a way to help children develop and learn? When you ask these questions, you are on the road to understanding and using the DEC Recommended Practices for interaction!

Characteristics of Adult-Child Interaction

Typical interactions with three children—a baby, a toddler, and a preschooler—can be used to illustrate not only how interactions with children differ from those with adults but also how interactions change over time in response to children's emerging abilities and changing interests.

Baby Joshua is sitting on his father's lap, looking at his father's face. Dad covers his eyes with his hand. "Where's Daddy?" Joshua looks expectantly at his father's face as his father pauses. He begins to wiggle. Suddenly his father withdraws his hand and says "Here he is!" Joshua squeals in delight. Then he stops and looks at his father. "Oh, you want me to do it again!" This continues for a few turns. Then Dad shifts the game, covering Joshua's eyes. "Where's Joshua?" He pauses. Joshua remains very still for a few seconds, then begins to move. Dad suddenly withdraws his hand and exclaims, "There he is!" while Joshua grins with delight. And the game continues until Joshua looks away toward the window. Dad raises him into the air and says, "That was fun! You really LIKE to play peekaboo!" and then puts him on the floor to crawl to the window.

Toddler Elizabeth is sitting on the floor, looking at a book. She is pointing toward pictures and talking to herself. She points, says a word, and looks toward her caregiver, Lupe, who is watching as she prepares a snack. Lupe smiles. "Yes, you found a cow! What else can you find in that book? Let me see, too!" Lupe moves over and sits down slightly behind and beside Elizabeth so they can both see the book. Elizabeth points and says, "Neighhh." Lupe responds, "Yes, that is a horse. A horse says neighhh. Look, the horse is eating hay." Elizabeth responds, "Horse hungry." "Yes, the horse must be hungry, because he is eating hay. Soon YOU will be hungry, too, and we will have our snack." Elizabeth looks at Lupe with a mischievous smile. "Me eat hay, too!"

Preschooler Liza is building a tower of blocks in the play area as Ted watches. "Your tower is getting really tall. I wonder how many blocks you can put on there before it falls." Liza continues to place blocks, periodically looking toward Ted. "Yes, I see that you are adding more blocks. Let's count how many you have so far." They count together. "How many more do you plan to add?" "Five." "Five more. . . . I think it will fall down before you get to five!" "I don't think so! Watch!" Liza continues to add blocks as Ted counts each one—1, 2, 3, 4, 5—and unobtrusively reaches to steady the blocks. "See, I did it!" "You certainly did! You made a tower that is almost as tall as you are! Shall we count again and see how many you have altogether?" "Yes! You help me."

As you reflected on your interaction with Gretchen, you identified several important components that apply to ALL interactions, including those with young children. These were a common topic, avenues used for interaction (verbal and nonverbal), and the alternating roles of listener and communicator. A reciprocal, shared interaction was accomplished because each of you attended to and responded to the signals of the other. Your individual streams of behavior took on a predictable turn-taking structure in which you each felt both competent and confident as interactors. Your interaction strengthened your relationship and made it likely that you would seek one another out again in the future.

Similar patterns of reciprocity were evident in each of the vignettes above, with similar consequences for the relationship. However, reciprocity was achieved differently with each of the three children. With a very young child such as Joshua, the joint "topic" of the interaction was shared emotion and enjoyment, accomplished through facial expression, vocalization, and movement rather than with words. While words were part of the interaction, the meaning was conveyed and shared in other ways. At this age, the roles of the two partners were also quite different; it was primarily the adult partner who fit in with and extended the child's participation and enjoyment, thereby establishing a turn-taking pattern. Through this pattern, Joshua will begin to learn that he has an effect on his partner and will begin to consciously engage in communicative behaviors. The enjoyment that each partner derived from the interaction also made it likely that this and other games and interactions will occur in the future.

Elizabeth's vignette reveals that she has already become more of an equal partner in the interaction than Joshua. Shared emotion is still an important feature (as it was with you and Gretchen), but because Elizabeth has become more interested in events in the world around her, Lupe is more likely to create an interaction by joining Elizabeth's focus of attention. At this age, the topic is more likely to be based on something that the child is interested in or engaged in beyond the adult, and the adult creates the interaction around that interest by responding to vocalizations or commenting on what the child is doing. Lupe also commented on her interpretation of what Elizabeth was feeling, matching and maintaining Elizabeth's emotional state. She also used much more language, re-

sponding but also extending with new language and ideas. Compared with the interaction with Joshua, this interaction has become more reliant on turn-taking via spoken language. Elizabeth is not yet an equal conversational partner; instead, Lupe creates interaction by using Elizabeth's focus to establish a shared focus and creating a structure for turn-taking around it. As above, the pleasure that each derived from the interaction is likely to lead each partner to seek out the other for future pleasurable interaction.

By the time she is a preschooler, Liza has many interests. She is curious about how things work and likes to explore ideas as well as the activities and objects she experiences. She engages in activities with her peers and has learned to engage in reciprocal play. She invites Ted into her play and responds to Ted's ideas and questions. As Ted joins Liza's play, he uses words for what she is thinking, doing, and feeling.

As he matches and helps to maintain Liza's enthusiasm, he also extends on her ideas and language. Liza has become a more equal interactional partner, taking responsibility for initiating interaction as well as for maintaining conversational turn-taking with Ted by responding to his comments and questions. Nevertheless, Ted, as the adult, is still the partner who carries most of the responsibility for keeping the interaction going by structuring it around Elizabeth's play and matching the positive emotional tone of the interaction.

These three interactions share similarities to one another as well as to the adult interaction described above. But there were also interesting differences in topic, in how the partners communicated, and in how reciprocity was accomplished as the adults shifted their roles in response to what their child partner brought to the interaction. Whereas babies express themselves (facially, bodily, vocally) primarily through emotions, older children increasingly use both verbal language and more finely tuned emotional expression. In all three vignettes, the adult and child shared a focus of attention. However, as the child developed, the focus began to shift from a primary emphasis on shared emotion to an interest in the external environment. At all three ages, the adult created an interaction context by joining the child's focus of attention. For older children, the ability to use verbal language, and the emerging ability to think and remember, make their interactions more like those of adults, although it is still the adult who is carrying most of the burden for identifying the interaction.

In all three vignettes, the positive emotion that was evident between adult and child kept the child in the interaction by eliciting enjoyment and feelings of being valued. In all three, adults added and expanded by slightly changing the rules to ask more of the child, or by adding in new content, first within a nonverbal game and then increasingly relying on new ideas and words. When needed, the adult added unobtrusive support or a new idea or modeled a new action that led the child toward more advanced behavior. Although adult roles shift over time as the adult adapts to the emerging abilities of the children, adults continue to carry the burden of making the interaction successful and emotionally satisfying, taking advantage of naturally occurring but changing opportunities as well as initiating new opportunities.

Throughout, the adult accomplishes what is often referred to as "responsive interaction" by adapting to changes in the communicative and other developmental abilities of the child, using multiple ways to achieve reciprocity and synchrony in the adult-child dyad. The keys to responsive interaction are the adult's sensitivity to the child's emotions and emerging abilities and responsiveness to the child's interests, emotions, and unintentional and intentional communicative acts.

Another key is that the child is able to perceive the relationship between what he is experiencing and the adult's response, or what is called "contingent responsiveness." For this to happen, the response must occur close in time to what the child is experiencing and also be matched to the child's experience so that the connection makes sense to the child.

Interaction and Children's Development and Learning

Each of the three vignettes above demonstrates how almost any example of pleasurable adult-child interaction simultaneously supports development and learning in language, cognitive, emotional, and social development. Within the context of each of the vignettes, the children experienced shared emotions that set the stage for their perceptions of self and others. They heard language that was closely linked to their thoughts and feelings. They experienced contingent responses that strengthened their actions and cognitions. They experienced opportunities and supports that led them toward more advanced behaviors and interactions.

It is not surprising that numerous developmental studies have linked aspects of responsive adult-child interaction (particularly sensitivity, responsiveness, and contingency) with many areas of development and learning in young children both with and without disabilities (Kassow & Dunst, 2007; Landry, Smith, & Swank, 2006; McCollum & Ostrosky, 2008; Nievar & Becker, 2007; Trivette, 2003; van IJzendoorn et al., 2007). The interactions that children experience early on also set the stage for the future emergence of more advanced abilities and skills.

> The keys to responsive interaction are the adult's sensitivity to the child's emotions and emerging abilities and responsiveness to the child's interests, emotions, and unintentional and intentional communicative acts.

Influence of Individual Differences on Quality of Interaction

Given that adult-child interaction occurs without conscious thought, why is it important to pay careful attention to the core components of interaction and think about how to use them as a key part of intervention with young children and their families? One important reason is that there are variations in adults' sensitivity and responsiveness, and these differences make a difference in children's outcomes. The interactions that different children experience, because they may differ in quality in relation to the characteristics described above, might over time be expected to lead to unintended differences in children's development and learning.

Another reason is that the natural flow of adult-child interactions can be disrupted when either the adult or the child bring individual differences to the interaction that may interfere with their ability to engage in responsive interaction. For example, particular life circumstances that create extreme stress for families, such as maternal depression, abuse, and parental lack of understanding of children's development, have all been found to be related to an adult's ability to establish mutually satisfying, developmentally promoting interactions with a child. Any of these factors may make it more difficult for adults to tune into and interpret the child's perspective or make it more difficult to regulate their behavior in response to the child.

Disruptions to mutually pleasurable interaction also can occur when children are not able to play their expected roles as interactive partners. What individual children bring to an interaction in the way of energy, emotional expression, or self-regulation may be influenced by factors such as prematurity or health. Children with specific disabilities may also bring different interaction abilities that require adults to go beyond what naturally happens because it may be more difficult for the adult to read the child's cues and to establish an interactive match. For example, a parent whose toddler is blind may have difficulty interpreting the child's interests and emotional signals because these differ from those of children who are typically developing. This parent may have to learn different ways of reading his or her child's interactive cues and find different ways of organizing their interactions with the child. Other disabilities such as autism, cerebral palsy, or Down syndrome may also disrupt the child's ability to engage in typical interactions and require additional effort on the part of the adult to recognize, interpret, and respond to communicative cues.

It is important to understand how individual differences in families, parents, or children may interfere with the ability of either partner to fulfill his or her role as an interactive partner and thus act as barriers to adult-child interaction. The characteristics of responsive interaction have been important components of many prevention and intervention programs for children and families in which barriers to interaction have been identified.

Responsive Interaction and Interaction Intervention

> It is important to understand how individual differences in families, parents, or children may interfere with the ability of either partner to fulfill their roles as interactive partners and thus act as barriers to adult-child interaction.

As you think about how early interactions relate to virtually all areas of development and learning and how certain individual differences in adults or children may interfere with the ability of an adult-child dyad to establish a mutually pleasurable, reciprocal interaction, you can begin to envision ways in which specific characteristics of responsive interaction might be important in early childhood practice, particularly given the characteristics of the children and families served in many child and family programs. You also think back to specific strategies that you learned about in school, such as following the child's lead and expanding children's language by adding in new ideas or words. You understand now that these are just different names for important aspects of responsive interaction.

The components of responsive interaction are important in at least two ways at the level of the individual practitioner. The first is in his or her interactions with young children. While practitioners cannot hope to have the same powerful influence as parents and other significant caregivers, they may be able to establish interactive patterns that provide opportunities for children to develop emotions, understandings, and behaviors that mitigate negative influences and put the child on a more typical developmental pathway. These new abilities may even influence other significant adults to engage in more developmentally supportive interactions.

The second way in which different components of responsive interaction are important to individual practitioners is in their roles in supporting parent-child relationships and providing opportunities for parents and other caregivers to learn new ways of interacting with children. Practitioners may be able to use what is often called "parent-mediated intervention" by pointing out the child's emerging abilities or how the child responds to the parent. For example, the interventionist working with the blind toddler and her parents might be able to identify different signals that the parents could use to interpret their baby's interests and emotions so they will be better able to create positive, reciprocal interactions.

Evaluation of prevention and intervention programs as well as individual research designed around the characteristics of developmentally promoting interactions indicate that adults (both parents and practitioners) can learn to consciously employ these characteristics as strategies in their interactions with young children (Dunst & Kassow, 2007; Girolametto, Weitzman, & Greenberg, 2003; Kong & Carta, 2011; Landry, Smith, Swank, Zucker, et al., 2012) and that their doing so is related to better outcomes for children of different ages and in different areas of development and learning (Dunst, Trivette, & Hamby, 2012; Landry, Smith, Swank, & Miller-Loncar, 2000; Warren & Brady, 2007). Based on these findings, researchers increasingly have begun to examine how teachers and other practitioners might be able to use some of the characteristics of responsive interactions in their work with children as well as in their work to support parents as mediators of their children's development and learning.

Achieving Responsive Interactions: The DEC Recommended Practices

The Interaction recommended practices encompass five responsive interaction practices that adults most often use unconsciously—but can also learn to employ consciously—to engage children in interactions that have qualities found to be related to important child outcomes. This set of five practices ensures that adults are physically and emotionally available to the child, highly sensitive to the child's nonverbal and verbal signals and interests, and able to adapt their interactions to match and respond to these signals and interests. Being emotionally and physically available and observing, interpreting, and responding are at the heart of

each of these five practices. Observation is key to interpreting the child's abilities and what the child is experiencing, whereas interpreting implies a conscious act on the part of the adult to understand the child's perspective in order to respond in ways that match and are contingent on the child's abilities, intent, and emotions.

The ability to interpret the child's perspective implies both a knowledge of the child's development (understandings, abilities) and a willingness to put oneself in the child's shoes to understand what the child is experiencing. Based on this interpretation, the adult then can join the child's focus of attention (e.g., reflect positive emotion, map language on the child's actions or interests, add new elements into a game). Thus, in each of the key practices, the adult waits, watches, interprets, and then acts in a way that is contingently matched to the child's focus so the child connects the response to his intentions and feelings. Very early in the child's life, for instance, what could be more matched and contingently responsive than simply imitating the child, which often leads to imitative turn-taking and much enjoyment? Later, what could be more matched and contingently responsive than simply commenting on what the child is doing, as he does it?

Explicit in three Interaction recommended practices, but also implied in two others, is the notion that responding to the child's cognitive and language activity should also include extending by adding new actions, information, and language, thereby adding new opportunities for development and learning. All five Interaction recommended practices are not only important for practitioners in their interactions with children but also as they work with other significant figures in the child's life to encourage use of the practices by all adults who engage with children. As illustrated in the vignettes, in interactions that are going well, these practices are naturally embedded throughout a child's day. The experience of predictable emotional, social, language, and cognitive responses also contributes naturally to progress in all areas of growth and learning.

Beyond the core components that apply across all five recommended practices, each of the recommended practices also provides examples of specific strategies to support the particular area of development. These specific strategies, like the practices themselves, are grounded in research in the particular area of development. For example, using language to label and expand on what the child is focusing on is more likely to lead to advanced language acquisition than other forms of language intervention. The practitioner who wants to foster problem-solving may observe to understand how a child is approaching a problem, interpret the child's thinking, and then respond by asking an open-ended question that pushes the child to a deeper level of thinking.

When children have specific areas of delay, the intervention may focus directly on observing, interpreting, responding, and scaffolding in relation to that particular area. For example, the practitioner who is concerned about language may observe for communicative attempts, interpret the child's intent, and then provide natural consequences and matched language for that intent (Girolametto, Verbey, & Tannock, 1994; Girolametto, Weitzman, & Greenberg, 2003). When children have disabilities often associated with delays in more than one area, such as autism, the intervention may focus on observing, interpreting, and following the child's lead across multiple areas of development (Schertz, Odom, Baggett, & Sideris, 2013). A similar, broader approach may also be appropriate when children are at risk because of family or parent factors (Landry, Smith, Swank, Zucker, et al., 2012). Both practitioners and parents can learn to use these practices, with beneficial outcomes for children.

Conclusions

Including "interaction" within the DEC Recommended Practices is a recognition of the powerful influence that early interactions have on children's development and learning, knowledge of the components of early interaction that are most likely to be associated with good outcomes for children, and knowledge of potential disruptions in establishing responsive interactions when children, parents, or families are experiencing factors that may interfere with responsive interaction. Increasingly, responsive interaction intervention is being used to ensure that the adults who interact with children do so in ways that incorporate these components. The core components are the same even though specific intervention programs or approaches may reflect the particular interest of the researcher (e.g., emotional development, language development) or may be geared toward the characteristics of particular groups of children (e.g., children with autism) or families (e.g., those with lower educational levels) or parents (e.g., mothers suffering from depression). While much of the research behind responsive interaction intervention is based on the characteristics of interactions between parents and their young children, the use of these practices is critical to practitioners as well,

In each of the key practices, the adult waits, watches, interprets, and then acts in a way that is contingently matched to the child's focus so the child connects the response to his intentions and feelings.

both as they interact with young children and as they provide parents and families with the support they need to aid the development of their children.

Humans are born to communicate, and many of the rhythms and ways of communicating that allow us to achieve the characteristics of responsive interaction are present from birth in all of us. While different cultures may guide the qualities of interaction in different ways, we all come into the world with a desire and need to interact, communicate, and develop reciprocal interactions and relationships with others. These relationships provide the framework for development in language and cognition as well as in later peer relationships and friendships. Within the context of our early interactions, we become good at understanding what others are conveying to us as well as conveying our thoughts and feelings to others. These interactions are critically important to early development. As shown in the DEC Recommended Practices, they can be taught, learned, and used in our work with children and families.

References

Dunst, C. J., & Kassow, D. Z. (2007). Characteristics of interventions promoting parental sensitivity to child behavior. *Winterberry Research Syntheses, 1*(13). Morganton, NC: Winterberry Press.

Dunst, C. J., Trivette, C. M., & Hamby, D. W. (2012). Effect of interest-based interventions on the social-communicative behavior of young children with autism spectrum disorders. *CELL Reviews, 5*(6). Morganton, NC: Center for Early Literacy Learning.

Girolametto, L., Verbey, M., & Tannock, R. (1994). Improving joint engagement in parent-child interaction: An intervention study. *Journal of Early Intervention, 18,* 155–167. doi:10.1177/105381519401800204

Girolametto, L., Weitzman, E., & Greenberg, J. (2003). Training day care staff to facilitate children's language. *American Journal of Speech-Language Pathology, 12,* 299–311. doi:10.1044/1058-0360(2003/076)

Kassow, D. Z., & Dunst, C. J. (2007). Relationship between parental contingent-responsiveness and attachment outcomes. *Winterberry Research Syntheses, 2*(1). Morganton, NC: Winterberry Press.

Kong, N. Y., & Carta, J. J. (2011). Responsive interaction interventions for children with or at risk for developmental delays: A research synthesis. *Topics in Early Childhood Special Education, 33,* 4–17. doi:10.1177/0271121411426486

Landry, S. H., Smith K. E., & Swank, P. R. (2006). Responsive parenting: Establishing early foundations for social, communication, and independent problem-solving skills. *Developmental Psychology, 42,* 627–642. doi:10.1037/0012-1649.42.4.627

Landry, S. H., Smith, K. E., Swank, P. R., & Miller-Loncar, C. L. (2000). Early maternal and child influences on children's later independent cognitive and social functioning. *Child Development, 71,* 358–375. doi:10.1111/1467-8624.00150

Landry, S. H., Smith, K. E., Swank, P. R., Zucker, T., Crawford, A. D., & Solari, E. F. (2012). The effects of a responsive parenting intervention on parent-child interactions during shared book reading. *Developmental Psychology, 48,* 969–986. doi:10.1037/a0026400

McCollum, J. A., & Ostrosky, M. M. (2008). Family roles in young children's emerging peer-related social competence. In W. H. Brown, S. L. Odom, & S. R. McConnell (Eds.), *Social competence of young children: Risk, disability, and intervention* (pp. 31–59). Baltimore, MD: Paul H. Brookes.

Nievar, M. A., & Becker, B. J. (2007). Sensitivity as a privileged predictor of attachment: A second perspective on De Wolff and van IJzendoorn's meta-analysis. *Social Development, 17*, 102–114. doi:10.1111/j.1467-9507.2007.00417.x

Schertz, H. H., Odom, S. L., Baggett, K. M., & Sideris, J. H. (2013). Effects of joint attention mediated learning (JAML) for toddlers with autistic spectrum disorders: An initial randomized controlled trial. *Early Childhood Research Quarterly, 28*, 249–258. doi:10.1016/j.ecresq.2012.06.006

Trivette, C. M. (2003). Influence of caregiver responsiveness on the development of young children with or at risk for developmental disabilities. *Bridges, 1*(3), 1–13.

Van IJzendoorn, M. H., Rutgers, A. H., Bakermans-Kranenburg, M. J., Swinkels, S. H. N., Van Daalen, E., Dietz, C., . . . Van Engeland, H. (2007). Parental sensitivity and attachment in children with autism spectrum disorder: Comparison with children with mental retardation, with language delays, and with typical development. *Child Development, 78*, 597–608. doi:10.1111/j.1467-8624.2007.01016.x

Warren, S. F., & Brady, N. C. (2007). The role of maternal responsivity in the development of children with intellectual disabilities. *Mental Retardation and Developmental Disabilities Research Reviews, 13*, 330–338. doi:10.1002/mrdd.20177

9

TEAMING AND COLLABORATION

Thinking About How as Well as What

CHELSEA GUILLEN
University of Illinois at Urbana-Champaign

PAM WINTON
University of North Carolina at Chapel Hill

TEAMING AND COLLABORATION IS A NEW TOPIC AREA FOR THE DEC Recommended Practices. We begin our discussion of these practices by providing background and the rationale for including this topic area. Following this, we provide definitions of the terminology used, a description of the five practices, including information about the evidence base tied to them, some examples of the practices being implemented, and a case vignette.

Background and Rationale

Though the themes reflected in these practices have been included in past versions of the DEC Recommended Practices, their presence here indicates recognition of a shift in how interventionists and educators do their work. These practices continue to highlight the importance of relationships, communication, and the use of collective wisdom for problem-solving when working with young children with disabilities and their families. For instance, the 2005 DEC Recommended Practices lists four theoretical principles for interdisciplinary practices. Two of these, *transdisciplinary* and *collective responsibility and teamwork*, are direct predecessors of this new topic area. A primary premise of the collective responsibility and teamwork principle is that decision-making is enhanced by the consideration of multiple perspectives. This is clearly a theme that is reinforced within the current Teaming and Collaboration recommended practices. A premise of the transdisciplinary principle was that there will be knowledge and competencies exchanged between team members. This theme is also reflected in the current Teaming and Collaboration recommended practices. In addition, the 2005 DEC Recommended Practices included a set of values and beliefs underlying all of the practices. One of these values was that families should receive high-quality, comprehensive, coordinated, and family-centered services and supports. This value could not be implemented without teaming and collaboration. So, though this is a new topic area, its roots have been deeply embedded in earlier versions of the recommended practices.

The 2014 DEC Recommended Practices are intended to represent the best available research as well as knowledge gained through experiences working with young children with disabilities and their families. While there is an emerging research base around teaming and collaboration in early childhood (Dinnebeil, Hale, & Rule, 1996, 1999; J. Olson, Murphy, & P. D. Olson, 1998), most of the research is qualitative with few rigorously designed experimental or quasi-experimental studies. Also, much of the literature reflects research that has been conducted in other fields such as business, social science, and organizational psychology. Further difficulty with gathering evidence around this topic area is related to the variety of terms used in the literature to describe the concepts and activities associated with both teaming and collaboration.

So, given its comparably smaller evidence base, why did the Recommended Practices Commission single out teaming and collaboration as a topic area? As stated in the preamble to this set of practices, "Educational programs and services for young children who have or are at risk for developmental delays and disabilities, by their nature, always involve more than one adult. The quality of the relationships and interactions among these adults affects the success of these programs" (Division for Early Childhood, 2014, p. 14). In addition, by legislative requirement (Individuals with Disabilities Education Act, 2004), teams in early intervention and early childhood special education always include at least an adult family member and a professional who supports the child and family.

Collaborative teaming is also seen as a critical component of successful inclusion (Hunt, Soto, Maier, Liboiron, & Bae, 2004). The expectation that professionals work together and with families has led to an evolution in the nature of practitioners' roles. McWilliam (2015) asserts that "the role of professionals in early intervention and early childhood special education has shifted from direct service to collaborative consultation" (p. 35). Given this shifting trend in how services are planned and delivered and its implications for how team members engage each other, detailing practices that address how parent-professional (as well as professional-professional) relationships can be established and nurtured is critical. Today's practitioners are expected to use a team-based approach that integrates the expertise of team members across disciplines and services to achieve child and family outcomes (Bruder & Dunst, 2005).

Terms and Guiding Principles

Having laid the foundation for why it is important to include the Teaming and Collaboration topic area in the 2014 DEC Recommended Practices, we will define key terms associated with each of the topic areas and related practices.[1] As mentioned earlier, one of the challenges inherent in this topic area is the lack of agreement and clarity on terms used in the literature, including the two terms that describe the topic area itself: *teaming* and *collaboration*.

For the purpose of the 2014 DEC Recommended Practices, a team includes "representatives from multiple disciplines and the family who join forces or combine efforts in response to the service setting, unique needs and desired outcomes of the child and family. Each individual on the team contributes to a clearly-defined portion of the effort" (Division for Early Childhood, 2014, p. 14). In other words, identifying and using the collective wisdom of the team rather than having a few strong voices dominate decisions is considered the essence of teamwork. The term *collaboration*, for the purposes of the 2014 DEC Recommended Practices, is defined as "interactive relationships between adults such as family members and professionals who work together to achieve mutually agreed upon outcomes/goals" (Division for Early Childhood, 2014). It is important to keep these terms and definitions in mind when considering the challenges inherent in reviewing the literature on teaming and collaboration.

Let us first review terminology related to teaming. Much of the teaming literature describes team organization, interaction structures, and approaches to service delivery. Frequently used terms in this area are *multidisciplinary, interdisciplinary, transdisciplinary*, and *primary service provider*. Woodruff and McGonigel (1988) provide a description of how multidisciplinary, interdisciplinary, and transdisciplinary team structures impact a number of tasks performed by early interventionists. On multidisciplinary teams, practitioners from multiple disciplines primarily work independently of each other. Interdisciplinary team practitioners establish formal opportunities for communication to share information and discuss service plans while still

maintaining responsibility for parts of the plan related to specific professional disciplines (e.g., a physical therapist addresses gross-motor outcomes). Transdisciplinary teams work to transcend the limits of their individual disciplines by committing to "cross and recross disciplinary boundaries" (p.167) for maximum communication, interaction, and cooperation among team members.

Shelden and Rush (2013) add to these descriptions by differentiating the primary service provider (PSP) approach from the transdisciplinary approach. They state that with the PSP approach, practitioners are not "asked to engage in role release and take on the role of practitioners from other disciplines" (p. 7). The PSP is expected to become familiar with the child's and family's activities, routines, and interests to promote the parent's ability to facilitate their child's participation in daily activities. Given these descriptions, it should be relatively easy to distinguish between the different teaming approaches and conduct research. In reality, however, a lack of agreement on these descriptions and the difficulty inherent in operationalizing these models for the purpose of research make it challenging to investigate.

Terminology related to collaboration also has some limitations. The term *collaboration* is sometimes used interchangeably in the literature with the term *coordination*. Hicks, Larson, Nelson, Olds, and Johnston (2008), however, offer a way to differentiate between the two activities. They assert that collaboration is more than just coordinating efforts toward a mutually desired outcome. Collaboration differs from coordination in that prior to the collaboration, no individual team member has *full* knowledge of either the problem or the solution. Collaboration helps teams clearly define the problem, set goals, establish a plan for reaching the goals, and reach agreement for team members' roles in executing the plan. Coordination, in contrast, often comes after collaboration; it describes team members working together in the most efficient and effective manner to achieve the desired outcome. Coordination presumes that the team has come to agreement on both the problem and the method for resolution. Though this work has largely focused on the effectiveness of home visiting programs, collaboration between team members has clear relevance for early intervention and early childhood special education.

Mattessich and Monsey (1992) conducted a review of the literature on the factors that influence successful collaborations. Their review was based on research with groups from a variety of arenas, including health and education. After synthesizing the information, 19 factors that influence successful collaboration were identified. Many of these factors have direct applicability to early intervention/early childhood special education practitioners' work and could be considered the guiding principles for successful collaboration. Factors from this list that are evident in the Teaming and Collaboration recommended practices relate to team composition (appropriate cross-section of members and a skilled convener), communication and group facilitation strategies (mutual respect, understanding and trust, ability to compromise, flexibility, adaptability, open and frequent communication), and team purpose (shared vision and concrete, attainable goals and objectives). Though research on collaboration is considered to be in its early stages, there is considerable support for the use of many of the strategies highlighted in these practices.

Practices and Examples

The practices in this topic area "promote and sustain collaborative adult partnerships, relationships, and ongoing interactions to ensure that programs and services achieve desired child and family outcomes and goals" (Division for

Early Childhood, 2014, p. 14). They include "strategies for interacting and sharing knowledge and expertise in ways that are respectful, supportive, enhance capacity, and are culturally sensitive" (p. 14). Given this information, the Teaming and Collaboration practices describe ways to support communication, to share knowledge, and to recognize and benefit from team members' unique assets and contributions to achieve a shared outcome. The practices, descriptions of the evidence, and examples of the practices being implemented can be found below.

TC1. Practitioners representing multiple disciplines and families work together as a team to plan and implement supports and services to meet the unique needs of each child and family. This practice highlights the overarching premise that practitioners will participate in teams with others who have varying experience and training. It is based on the assumption that groups who pool their collective expertise are more effective at addressing the challenges that young children with disabilities and their families encounter. Teams may vary in size depending on their tasks and contexts. The evidence the Gap Analysis Group cited in support of this particular practice primarily comes from the fields of organizational science and business. The studies cited as providing evidence for this practice examined a number of variables that impacted the success and effectiveness of teams (Cohen & Bailey, 1997; Hackman, 1987; Hoegl & Gemuenden, 2001; West, Brodbeck, & Richter, 2004). A couple of examples:

> A physical therapist and special instructor meet to talk with the family about the child's current abilities and progress and modify current strategies to align with the child's current level of performance.

> An early childhood teacher discusses her ideas and concerns about a child's progress with the consulting speech language pathologist, and they develop additional teaching strategies.

Being emotionally and physically available and observing, interpreting, and responding are at the heart of each of these five practices.

TC2. Practitioners and families work together as a team to systematically and regularly exchange expertise, knowledge, and information to build team capacity and jointly solve problems, plan, and implement interventions. This practice moves beyond the presumption that practitioners will work on teams and describes the expectations for what team members will do in support of the team. The cited studies that support this practice were conducted in the fields of early intervention and early childhood special education and include a variety of methods for examining the topic. Much of the evidence comes from examining the use of coaching strategies with caregivers (Friedman, Woods, & Salisbury, 2012; Kaminski, Valle, Filene, & Boyle, 2008; Peterson, Luze, Eshbaugh, Jeon, & Kantz, 2007) and other professionals (Fox, Hemmeter, Snyder, Binder, & Clarke, 2011; McCollum, Hemmeter, & Hsieh, 2013; Neuman & Cunningham, 2009) to improve social interactions (Mahoney & Perales, 2005). A few examples:

> An early childhood teacher participates in the child's monthly team meetings convened by the service coordinator to discuss progress and share ideas for supporting goals in the classroom setting.

A family child care teacher spends a few minutes at pickup and dropoff to exchange information about the child's performance with the family.

An itinerant teacher works with the classroom teacher to model and demonstrate a strategy to support a child's development and learning during outdoor play.

TC3. Practitioners use communication and group facilitation strategies to enhance team functioning and interpersonal relationships with and among team members. This practice highlights a variety of strategies that have been associated with improved relationships among team members. Evidence for this practice comes from a variety of fields, including psychology, education, leadership, medicine, and rehabilitation. This group of primarily descriptive, correlational, and quasi-experimental studies has looked at various aspects of team member attributes (Bell, 2007), program attributes (Dinnebeil et al., 1999), communication and group facilitation including team functioning (Flowers, Mertens & Mulhall, 1999), decision-making (Hunt et al., 2004), and team leadership/supervisor training (Hundert & Hopkins, 1992; West, Borrill et al., 2003). Based on this work, we know that being intentional about team composition and promoting opportunities for communication has positive effects on outcomes, team morale, and team satisfaction. A couple of examples:

A program director acknowledges gaps in communication among teachers and teacher aides and develops a plan to remedy the problems.

A team leader uses a round robin technique in a group meeting to ensure that each member of the team, including those who typically are quiet, has a chance to express their perspectives and ideas on an issue.

TC4. Team members assist each other to discover and access community-based services and other informal and formal resources to meet family-identified child or family needs. This practice speaks to the importance of team members not only exchanging information for problem-solving and intervention planning but also for identifying informal and formal resources to address families' needs and interests. There was no validated evidence for this practice, but professional wisdom suggests its value because supports in both early intervention and early childhood special education are intended to be individualized. It is unreasonable to expect any one family or team member to be aware of all the resources available in a given community. The sharing of information among team members regarding both needs and resources increases the likelihood that families will be able to access the supports they find most useful. A few examples:

> A service coordinator learns about reimbursement policies and helps other team members, as needed, to understand the impact of using nonpublic funds to pay for services.

> A social worker compiles a resource book on programs, funding options, and policies.

> A case manager invites contributions and perspectives of each team member about placement options to meet a child's and family's needs.

TC5. Practitioners and families may collaborate with each other to identify one practitioner from the team who serves as the primary liaison between the family and other team members based on child and family priorities and needs. This practice highlights the importance of designating a team member to facilitate team communication. The evidence cited in support of this practice comes primarily from a correlational study conducted in the United Kingdom (Sloper, Greco, Beecham & Webb, 2006), where the presence of key workers was associated with better care coordination for young children with disabilities and their families. Professionals' support for this practice can be found in the key principles for providing early intervention services in natural environments developed by OSEP's Technical Assistance Community of Practice: Part C Settings (Workgroup on Principles and Practices in Natural Environments, 2008). This practice is also consistent with the organizational makeup of many early childhood classrooms where the teacher serves as the primary contact between families and other service providers. A couple of examples:

> During a home visit, the occupational therapist shares strategies with parents that were developed in conjunction with the physical therapist.

> An early childhood teacher, who serves as the primary contact for the family, receives instruction, feedback, and support from the itinerant hearing specialist in order to provide individualized support for the child within the classroom.

> We know that being intentional about team composition and promoting opportunities for communication has positive effects on outcomes, team morale, and team satisfaction.

Case Vignette: Putting the Practices Into Action

Kelly, a 12-month-old who has Down syndrome, receives early intervention services. Kelly's parents recently moved to be closer to their extended family. Because of Kelly's individual needs, Kelly and her family are supported by a team that includes a service coordinator, a special instructor, a speech-language pathologist, a physical therapist, and an occupational therapist. The family's recent move, in addition to Kelly's medical needs and ongoing visits with specialists, prompted her parents to ask their team for a way to minimize the number of intervention visits received each week while maximizing their ability to access the support and information needed to facilitate Kelly's development.

Kelly's parents shared their concerns and priorities for Kelly. Their current priority is for Kelly to find an effective way to move about her environment. They know that her ability to explore the world around her will positively impact her global development as well as her independence.

Based on this priority and the expertise of the team members, the physical therapist is selected to serve as the primary service provider. She visits the family weekly, collecting information about the family's routines and interests and providing information to Kelly's parents about how to facilitate movement during these routines. The physical therapist also meets with team members each month to provide updates on what she learns from the family and on Kelly's progress toward her outcome.

When Kelly's parents request support as they transition Kelly to table foods,

the physical therapist asks them if she could invite the speech language pathologist to her next visit. They agree and plan for a co-visit. During that visit, Kelly's parents talk with both practitioners about what foods they have successfully and unsuccessfully tried and show them how they have been feeding Kelly. Based on this information, the practitioners share some strategies that the parents can try and agree to discuss this information with the other team members.

After the next team meeting, the physical therapist brings an adaptive spoon that the occupational therapist felt could help with Kelly's independent feeding and a resource on transitioning to table foods that the special instructor provided. She also asked Kelly's parents about extended family members who might be involved in feeding Kelly to ensure that everyone has the information and resources they need when Kelly is in their care. They try the new spoon during the visit and make revisions to the strategies the family has tried. The physical therapist makes sure to share information about the family's successes and challenges during the next team meeting.

Note

1. Terms used in the DEC Recommend Practices are available online (Division for Early Childhood, 2014).

References

Bell, S. T. (2007). Deep-level composition variables as predictors of team performance: A meta-analysis. *Journal of Applied Psychology, 92,* 595–615. doi:10.1037/0021-9010.92.3.595

Bruder, M. B., & Dunst, C. J. (2005). Personnel preparation in recommended early intervention practices: Degree of emphasis across disciplines. *Topics in Early Childhood Special Education, 25,* 25–33. doi:10.1177/02711214050250010301

Cohen, S. G., & Bailey, D. E. (1997). What makes teams work: Group effectiveness research from the shop floor to the executive suite. *Journal of Management, 23,* 239–290. doi:10.1177/014920639702300303

Dinnebeil, L. A., Hale, L. M., & Rule, S. (1996). A qualitative analysis of parents' and service coordinators' descriptions of variables that influence collaborative relationships. *Topics in Early Childhood Special Education, 16,* 322–347. doi:10.1177/027112149601600305

Dinnebeil, L. A., Hale, L., & Rule, S. (1999). Early intervention program practices that support collaboration. *Topics in Early Childhood Special Education, 19,* 225–235. doi:10.1177/027112149901900403

Division for Early Childhood. (2014). *DEC recommended practices in early intervention/early childhood special education 2014.* Retrieved from http://www.dec-sped.org/recommendedpractices

Flowers, N., Mertens, S. B., & Mulhall, P. F. (1999). The impact of teaming: Five research-based outcomes. *Middle School Journal, 31*(1), 57–60.

Fox, L., Hemmeter, M. L., Snyder, P., Binder, D. P., & Clarke, S. (2011). Coaching early childhood special educators to implement a comprehensive model for promoting young children's social competence. *Topics in Early Childhood Special Education, 31,* 178–192. doi:10.1177/0271121411404440

Friedman, M., Woods, J., & Salisbury, C. (2012). Caregiver coaching strategies for early intervention providers: Moving toward operational definitions. *Infants & Young Children, 25,* 62–82. doi:10.1097/IYC.0b013e31823d8f12

Hackman, J. R. (1987). The design of work teams. In J. W. Lorsch (Ed.), *Handbook of organizational behavior* (pp. 315–342). Englewood Cliffs, NJ: Prentice-Hall.

Hicks, D., Larson, C., Nelson, C., Olds, D. L., & Johnston, E. (2008). The influence of collaboration on program outcomes: The Colorado nurse-family partnership. *Evaluation Review, 32,* 453–477. doi:10.1177/0193841X08315131

Hoegl, M., & Gemuenden, H. G. (2001). Teamwork quality and the success of innovative projects: A theoretical concept and empirical evidence. *Organization Science, 12,* 435–449. doi:10.1287/orsc.12.4.435.10635

Hundert, J., & Hopkins, B. (1992). Training supervisors in a collaborative team approach to promote peer interaction of children with disabilities in integrated preschools. *Journal of Applied Behavior Analysis, 25,* 385–400. doi:10.1901/jaba.1992.25-385

Hunt, P., Soto, G., Maier, J., Liboiron, N., & Bae, S. (2004). Collaborative teaming to support preschoolers with severe disabilities who are placed in general education early childhood programs. *Topics in Early Childhood Special Education, 24,* 123–142. doi:10.1177/02711214040240030101

Individuals with Disabilities Education Act, 20 U.S.C. § 1400 (2004).

Kaminski, J. W., Valle, L. A., Filene, J. H., & Boyle, C. L. (2008). A meta-analytic review of components associated with parent training program effectiveness. *Journal of Abnormal Psychology, 36,* 567–589. doi:10.1007/s10802-007-9201-9

Mahoney, G., & Perales, F. (2005). Relationship-focused early intervention with children with pervasive developmental disorders and other disabilities: A comparative study. *Journal of Developmental and Behavioral Pediatrics, 26,* 77–85.

Mattessich, P. W., & Monsey, B. R. (1992). *Collaboration: What makes it work.* St. Paul, MN: Amherst H. Wilder Foundation.

McCollum, J. A., Hemmeter, M. L., & Hsieh, W.-Y. (2013). Coaching teachers for emergent literacy instruction using performance-based feedback. *Topics in Early Childhood Special Education, 33,* 28–37. doi:10.1177/0271121411431003

McWilliam, R. A. (2015). Future of early intervention with infants and toddlers for whom typical experiences are not effective. *Remedial and Special Education, 36,* 33–38. doi:10.1177/0741932514554105

Neuman, S. B., & Cunningham, L. (2009). The impact of professional development and coaching on early language and literacy instructional practices. *American Educational Research Journal, 46,* 532–566. doi:10.3102/0002831208328088

Olson, J., Murphy, C. L., & Olson, P. D. (1998). Building effective successful teams: An interactive teaming model for inservice education. *Journal of Early Intervention, 21,* 339–349. doi:10.1177/105381519802100407

Peterson, C. A., Luze, G. J., Eshbaugh, E. M., Jeon, H.-J., & Kantz, K. R. (2007). Enhancing parent-child interactions through home visiting: Promising practice or unfulfilled promise? *Journal of Early Intervention, 29,* 119–140. doi:10.1177/105381510702900205

Shelden, M. L., & Rush, D. D. (2013). *The early intervention teaming handbook: The primary service provider approach.* Baltimore, MD: Paul H. Brookes.

Sloper, P., Greco, V., Beecham, J., & Webb, R. (2006). Key worker services for disabled children: What characteristics of services lead to better outcomes for children and families? *Child: Care, Health and Development, 32,* 147–157. doi:10.1111/j.1365-2214.2006.00592.x

West, M. A., Borrill, C. S., Dawson, J. F., Brodbeck, F., Shapiro, D. A., & Haward, B. (2003). Leadership clarity and team innovation in health care. *The Leadership Quarterly, 14,* 393–410.

West, M. A., Brodbeck, F. C., & Richter, A. W. (2004). Does the "romance of teams" exist? The effectiveness of teams in experimental and field settings. *Journal of Occupational and Organization Psychology, 77,* 467–473. doi:10.1348/0963179042596450

Woodruff, G., & McGonigel, M. (1988). Early intervention team approaches: The transdisciplinary model. In J. B. Jordan, J. J. Gallagher, P. L. Hutinger, & M. B. Karnes (Eds.), *Early childhood special education: Birth to three* (pp. 163–181). Reston, VA: Council for Exceptional Children.

Workgroup on Principles and Practices in Natural Environments, OSEP TA Community of Practice: Part C Settings. (2008, March). *Agreed upon mission and key principles for providing early intervention services in natural environments.* Retrieved from http://ectacenter.org/~pdfs/topics/families/Finalmissionandprinciples3_11_08.pdf

10

TRANSITION

Using the Recommended Practices to Support Continuity and Transitions

BETH S. ROUS
University of Kentucky

FOR YOUNG CHILDREN WITH DISABILITIES, SUPPORTING THEIR TRANsition between and among services, supports, and programs is a major component of the service system. Transition planning is a requirement for children participating in early intervention services through Part C and Head Start programs. Although transition has been a topic of interest and focus for many years, early intervention and early childhood special educators often continue to struggle with supporting children and families through the transition process (Hanson et al., 2000; Rous, Myers, & Sticklin, 2007). This article will present components of transition planning within the context of larger system changes in early care, education, and intervention; key elements of transition planning; and guidance for using the Transition recommended practices.

Transition Planning Amid the Changing Context of Early Childhood Education

The early childhood system has undergone massive changes in the last decade with increases in the investment in early childhood services and supports (e.g., Race to the Top – Early Learning Challenge). These investments have focused on increasing the quality of the early care and education environments (i.e., tiered quality rating and improvement systems), integration and coordination across the early childhood sectors (i.e., child care, Head Start, and public PreK), integration of professional development systems and investments in the workforce, and more accountability for child outcomes (i.e., school readiness). These initiatives have created both opportunities and challenges for young children with disabilities, specifically related to their transition between and among programs.

Critical Components of Transition Planning

Early childhood educators have becoming increasingly aware of the importance of continuity of care in the lives of young children (Shonkoff & Phillips, 2000), specifically related to the care of infants and toddlers (Kochanska, Murray, & Harlan, 2000) and young children with disabilities (Kemp, 2003; Le Ager & Shapiro, 1995; Love, Logue, Trudeau, & Thayer, 1992). As a result, the identification of practices to support children's transitions between and among programs has become critical to supporting continuity of care, especially for children with or at-risk for disabilities.

To best understand and support transitions, it is helpful to review and define common terms often used to describe and report research across the fields of early childhood and early childhood special education (Rous & Hallam, 2012; Rous & Mawdsley, in press). Common terms include *transition, continuity,* and *alignment.*

Transition has often been described in the literature as a change in settings within a period of time, such as a day (Kagan, 1991), and/or across time, such  as the move from early intervention services to preschool services to kindergarten (Daley, Munk, & Carlson, 2011; Rous, Hallam, Harbin, McCormick, & Jung, 2007). Using this definition, the actual transition is limited to the time it takes for a child to make the move across settings. In reality, children move between programs and settings from one day to the next or, in the case of preschool or kindergarten, often at the end of the summer. Therefore, a bigger component of the transition process is the degree to which children and their families are prepared for the "move" and are able to adjust to the "move" among settings, providers, programs, etc. (Rous, Hallam, Harbin, et al., 2007). This preparation and adjustment can be supported by attending to the continuity and alignment among settings.

Continuity was defined by Bredekamp (2010) as the "coherence and connectedness among a child's experiences at home and school from preschool through the elementary grades" (p. 135). For young children with disabilities, continuity should also be considered between early intervention and preschool programs. Another way to think about continuity is the degree to which transparent and concrete connections can be made between programs and settings so children are able to adjust more quickly after the transition. When these connections are not made at the program, classroom, and individual levels, discontinuity occurs (Love et al., 1992). In the case of a young child with a disability, examples can include differences in interventions (e.g., strategies practitioners use to support the child's learning and development, goals, and outcomes) and/or accommodations, adaptations, or modifications to the environment (e.g., communication device, classroom setup).

The other important component of transition planning is alignment. Kagan and Kaurez (2007) discussed alignment as the correspondence among early learning standards (what children are expected to learn), curriculum (what is taught), and assessment (how learning is evaluated). At a most basic level, alignment helps ensure teachers are able to focus on congruent instructional practices across settings to support consistent developmental goals and outcomes identified for children (Hair, Halle, Terry-Humen, Lavelle, & Calkins, 2006). When misalignment occurs, children may be exposed to different and often conflicting instruction and interventions.

Implementing the Recommended Practices for Transition

The Division for Early Childhood (2014) identified two key practices to support better transition experiences for young children with disabilities and their families. Across both practices, there are three critical elements: timing of the practice, practitioner role, and impact of the practice on the child's adjustment and child outcomes. In addition, the practices focus on two key aspects of the transition process: communication and planned and timely strategies. Therefore, to effectively implement the practices, one must understand the critical elements and aspects embedded in the two Transition recommended practices (p. 15).

Timing of the Practice

Each recommended practice addresses three key time points in the transition process: before, during, and after. Strategies implemented before the transition are designed to support the preparation of children and families for the move to a new setting or program. The timing of implementation of these strategies is dependent on the "goal" of the strategy. For example, helping the child learn specific skills needed in a new environment (e.g., following directions, navigating family-style meals) may take months or weeks depending on the child's developmental status and the skill set required.

On the other hand, connecting families with a new teacher or service provider is dependent on when decisions are made about placement of children in a new program. The timing of preparation activities is also dependent on the transition point. Transitioning from early intervention programs to preschool programs must be completed by the child's third birthday; the transition from preschool to kindergarten programs is most often based on the school calendar.

Strategies used during the transition process are focused on the short period of time when the change in settings actually occurs. These strategies are designed to ensure the child and family can navigate the actual move. For example, knowing when the bus will pick up the child and the start and ending times for the program, negotiating the transfer of records and/or materials, and providing information on how parents are involved in the program all must be handled "during" the actual transition. The timing of these strategies can span a

The identification of practices to support children's transitions between and among programs has become critical to supporting continuity of care, especially for children with or at-risk for disabilities.

day, a week, or a few months in the case of summer breaks for public preschool and kindergarten programs.

Strategies used after the transition process focus on child and family adjustment to the new program or setting. These strategies are generally implemented during the first few days or weeks after a child starts a program. They are designed to help ensure the child successfully engages in the new environment and can adapt to both the structure and culture of that environment (Rous, Harbin & McCormick, 2006).

Practitioner Role in the Transition

Regardless of the program in which they work, practitioners support multiple transitions for the children and families they serve. These roles are typically described as "sending" and "receiving." Practitioners in early intervention serve in the "receiving" role as infants and toddlers are referred to early intervention and begin receiving services. In this case, providers often have little time to support the preparation of children and families for the transition, focusing more on the "during" transition time point. Once the child begins receiving early intervention services, the practitioner stays in the "receiving role" and supports the child's adjustment to the program. They then move into a "sending" role, where they identify strategies and supports to "prepare" children to transition out of the program at age 3 (or when they achieve the outcomes and goals outlined on their IFSP). Table 1 provides an example of the timing and role of the early intervention provider throughout a child's participation in early intervention services.

Table 1
Practitioner Role in the Transition

	Transition time point	Goal	EI practitioner role
Referral to EI	During	Move into the program	Receiving
First few weeks in program	After	Adjustment	Receiving
Receiving services	Before	Preparation	Sending
Prior to age 3, referral to preschool	During	Move into a new program	Sending
Receiving services	After	Adjustment	Sending

Impact of the Practice on the Child's Adjustment and Child Outcomes

The ultimate goal of good transition planning is a child's timely and successful adjustment into a new setting or program. As described by Rous, Harbin, & McCormick (2006), this includes the child's ability to engage socially with peers and adults in the new setting. They must also be able to engage in the physical environment, either through the design of the classroom and/or through the use of accommodations or adaptions. Successful adjustment also includes the ability of the child to quickly adapt to the structure of the classroom (e.g., routines, activities, curricula) as well as the culture of the classroom (e.g., written and unwritten rules). This successful engagement and adaptation should support the child's continued growth and development.

Research is emerging to support the connection between good transition planning and later child outcomes. Early research has found positive relationships between the use of developmentally appropriate practices at the preschool and kindergarten levels and better academic outcomes in later grades (Entwisle & Alexander, 1998; Greenberg et al., 1999; Huffman & Spear, 2000; Mantzicopoulos, 2005; Marcon, 2002). More recent studies have focused on the connections between specific transition practices and later academic achievement (LoCasale-Crouch, Mashburn, Downer, & Pianta, 2008; Schulting, Malone & Dodge, 2005). These practices include simple strategies such as sending information home to parents about new programs and classroom visits by children and families before the transition occurs.

Communication Between Practitioners

The first of the two key aspects of the transition process addressed in the recommended practices is communication. Communication between and among early care and education providers serving children with disabilities is critical to supporting the transition process across time points. During transitions, informational exchanges are important for both the preparation of the child and family as well as their adjustment to the new program or setting.

Communication channels require an infrastructure through which practitioners can develop relationships and share information either within programs, such as the transition from public PreK to kindergarten, and/or across programs, such as the transition from early intervention to preschool (Bruder & Bologna, 1993; Rosenkoetter, Hains, & Fowler, 1994; Rous, Myers, & Stricklin, 2007; Rous,

Hemmeter, & Schuster, 1999).

Numerous strategies have appeared in the literature to support cross-agency/program communication. Most common are interagency agreements (Fowler & McCollum, 2000). Interagency agreements or memoranda of understanding (MOUs) can be helpful in outlining information that can be regularly shared between practitioners before, during, and after the transition. These agreements should delineate and clarify the roles and responsibilities of practitioners in this process. Other strategies can include opportunities for practitioners across programs to meet to share ideas, discuss challenges, and identify specific strategies to better support the transition process for children and families.

To support the transition of children and families, receiving practitioners can provide information about their expectations within the new program. This

Table 2
Implementing Planful and Timely Transition Sample Strategies

Strategy	Purpose	When	Transition Goal	Practitioner Role
Transition plan	Individualized plan that includes activities to support a child's move into a new program.	Before the transition	Support preparation	Sending: Develop and implement the plan
Child transition profile	Individualize profile with information about the child's developmental status related to communication, classroom skills, and motor and health to support their engagement and adaptation to a new setting.	Before the transition	Support adjustment	Sending: Develop the profile and share with receiving agency
Home visits	Practitioner visits family and child in the home	Before the transition	Support preparation	Receiving: Arrange and implement the visit
		After the transition	Support adjustment	
Classroom visits	Children and families visit future settings	Before the transition	Support preparation	Sending: Arrange a visit in collaboration with receiving program/staff
Phase in days	Gradual transition of the child into a program based on a set schedule (e.g., increase time per day over a few weeks; increase days per week over a few weeks).	After the transition	Support adjustment	Receiving: Work with family to identify schedule

More information on these strategies can be found in Rous, Hallam, Turnbull, Buysse, and Winton (2010).

includes the daily schedule, routines and activities, specific curricula and assessments used, and the general outlay of the classroom and other environments in which children spend time. For sending agencies, sharing information about children who will be transitioning to the new program can help receiving teachers better plan the environment, activities, and routines. Sharing copies of the child's current IFSP (or IEP) in advance can help receiving teachers understand the child's goals, developmental status, and targeted interventions and services the child has been receiving.

Planned and Timely Strategies

The second key aspect addressed in the recommended practices is planned and timely strategies. This is in keeping with the concept of "intentionality" in teaching, whereby practitioners use a "planful, thoughtful, and purposeful" process to organize learning for the children they serve (Epstein, 2007, p. 1). The terms *practice* and *strategy* are often used interchangeably in the transition literature. To better support implementation, Rous (2008) proposes differentiating the two concepts, where a practice represents broad, global elements while strategies represent the practice in action and thus can be tailored to meet the individual needs of children, families, and/or the program. There are two types of transition strategies presented in the literature (Daley et al., 2011; Pianta, Cox, Taylor, & Early, 1999; Rous, Hallam, McCormick, & Cox, 2010). High-intensity strategies are those that involve individualization at the child and/or family levels (e.g., one-on-one meetings, classroom visits) while low-intensity strategies are those that involve groups (e.g., group classroom visits, open houses, form letters). Not surprisingly, preschool teachers report using low-intensity strategies more often than high-intensity one (Daley et al., 2011; Rous, Hallam, McCormick, et al., 2010).

Choosing appropriate strategies to support transitions for young children and families requires the practitioner to consider the "timing" of the practice (before, during, after) and its role (sending or receiving). In fact, many transition strategies described in the literature are consistent with good early childhood practice, yet the timing of the strategy allows it to be classified as a "transition strategy." For example, a home visit conducted immediately before a child's transition can support his or her preparation, while a home visit immediately after a child's transition can support his or her adjustment if the home visit is planned effectively. Table 2 presents a set of strategies identified through CONNECT: The Center to Mobilize Early Childhood Knowledge (Rous, Hallam, Turnbull, Buysse, & Winton, 2010) to support a "planned and timely" transition process. Additional supports and information about these strategies can be found on the CONNECT website (http://community.fpg.unc.edu/connect-modules/learners/module-2).

Children at-risk for and with disabilities often experience frequent transitions as they navigate the various services and supports designed to address their developmental needs (Hanson et al., 2000). Often, these transitions are more intense than those experienced by families of children without disabilities (Rous, Myers, & Stricklin, 2007). Therefore, specific attention to the implementation of

> Choosing appropriate strategies to support transitions for young children and families requires the practitioner to consider the "timing" of the practice (before, during, after) and its role (sending or receiving).

transition practices and strategies in a thoughtful and planful way can facilitate more successful and positive experiences as children move into new programs and settings.

References

Bredekamp, S. (2010). Aligning curriculum and teaching: A child focused approach. In S. L. Kagan & K. Tarrant (Eds.), *Transitions for young children: Creating connections across early childhood systems* (pp. 135–146). Baltimore, MD: Paul H. Brookes.

Bruder, M. B., & Bologna, T. (1993). Collaboration and service coordination for effective early intervention. In W. Brown, S. K. Thurman, & L. F. Pearl (Eds.), *Family-centered early intervention with infants and toddlers: Innovative cross-disciplinary approaches* (pp. 103–127). Baltimore, MD: Paul H. Brookes.

Daley, T. C., Munk, T., & Carlson, E. (2011). A national study of kindergarten transition practices for children with disabilities. *Early Childhood Research Quarterly, 26,* 409–419. doi:10.1016/j.ecresq.2010.11.001

Division for Early Childhood. (2014). *DEC recommended practices in early intervention/early childhood special education.* Retrieved from http://www.dec-sped.org/recommendedpractices

Entwisle, D. R., & Alexander, K. L. (1998). Facilitating the transition to first grade: The nature of transition and research on factors affecting it. *Elementary School Journal, 98,* 351–364.

Epstein, A. S. (2007). *The intentional teacher: Choosing the best strategies for young children's learning.* Washington, DC: National Association for the Education of Young Children.

Fowler, S. A., & McCollum, J. A. (2000). Supports and barriers to writing an interagency agreement on the preschool transition. *Journal of Early Intervention, 23,* 294–307. doi:10.1177/105381510002300040801

Greenberg, M. T., Lengua, L. J., Coie, J. D., Pinderhughes, E. E., Bierman, K., Dodge, K. A. . . . McMahon, R. J. (1999). Predicting developmental outcomes at school entry using a multiple-risk model: Four American communities. *Developmental Psychology, 35,* 403–417. doi:10.1037/0012-1649.35.2.403

Hair, E., Halle, T., Terry-Humen, E., Lavelle, B., & Calkins, J. (2006). Children's school readiness in the ECLS-K: Predictions to academic, health, and social outcomes in first grade. *Early Childhood Research Quarterly, 21,* 431–454. doi:10.1016/j.ecresq.2006.09.005

Hanson, M. J., Beckman, P. J., Horn, E., Marquart, J., Sandall, S. R., Greig, D., & Brennan, E. (2000). Entering preschool: Family and professional experiences in this transition process. *Journal of Early Intervention, 23,* 279–293. doi:10.1177/105381510002300040701

Huffman, L. R., & Speer, P. W. (2000). Academic performance among at-risk children: The role of developmentally appropriate practices. *Early Childhood Research Quarterly, 15,* 167–184. doi:10.1016/S0885-2006(00)00048-X

Kagan, S. L. (1991). Moving from here to there: Rethinking continuity and transitions in early care and education. In B. Spodek & O. Saracho (Eds.), *Yearbook in early childhood education* (Vol. 2, pp. 132–151). New York, NY: Teachers College Press.

Kagan, S. L. & Kaurez, K. (2007). Reaching for the whole: Integration and alignment in early education policy. In R. C. Pianta, M. J. Cox, & K. L. Snow (Eds.), *School readiness and the transition to kindergarten in the era of accountability* (pp. 11–30). Baltimore, MD: Paul H. Brookes.

Kemp, C. (2003). Investigating the transition of young children with intellectual disabilities into mainstream classes: An Australian perspective. *International Journal of Disability, Development and Education, 50*, 403–433. doi:10.1080/1034912032000155194

Kemp, C., & Carter, M. (2000). Demonstration of classroom survival skills in kindergarten: A five-year transition study of children with intellectual disabilities. *Educational Psychology, 20*, 393–411. doi:10.1080/713663756

Kochanska, G., Murray, K. T., & Harlan, E. T. (2000). Effortful control in early childhood: Continuity and change, antecedents, and implications for social development. *Developmental Psychology, 36*, 220–232. doi:10.1037/0012-1649.36.2.220

Le Ager, C., & Shapiro, E. S. (1995). Template matching as a strategy for assessment of and intervention for preschool students with disabilities. *Topics in Early Childhood Special Education, 15*, 187–218. doi:10.1177/027112149501500204

LoCasale-Crouch, J., Mashburn, A. J., Downer, J. T., & Pianta, R. C. (2008). Pre-kindergarten teachers' use of transition practices and children's adjustment to kindergarten. *Early Childhood Research Quarterly, 23*, 124–139. doi:10.1016/j.ecresq.2007.06.001

Love, J. M., Logue, M. E., Trudeau, J. V., & Thayer, K. (1992). *Transitions to kindergarten in American schools: Final report of the national transition study*. Portsmouth, NH: RMC Research Corp. Retrieved from http://files.eric.ed.gov/fulltext/ED344693.pdf

Mantzicopoulos, P. (2005). Conflictual relationships between kindergarten children and their teachers: Associations with child and classroom context variables. *Journal of School Psychology, 43*, 425–442. doi:10.1016/j.jsp.2005.09.004

Marcon, R. A. (2002). Moving up the grades: Relationship between preschool model and later school success. *Early Childhood Research & Practice, 4*(1). Retrieved from http://ecrp.uiuc.edu/v4n1/marcon.html

Pianta, R. C., Cox, M. J., Taylor, L., & Early, D. (1999). Kindergarten teachers' practices related to the transition to school: Results of a national survey. *Elementary School Journal, 100*, 71–86.

Rosenkoetter, S. E., Hains, A. H., & Fowler, S. A. (1994). *Bridging early services for children with special needs and their families: A practical guide for transition planning*. Baltimore, MD: Paul H. Brookes.

Rous, B. (2008). *Recommended transition practices for young children and families: Results from a national validation survey* (Technical Report #3). Lexington: University of Kentucky, Human Development Institute, National Early Childhood Transition Center. Retrieved from http://www.hdi.uky.edu/for-professionals

Rous, B. S., & Hallam, R. A. (2012). Transition services for children with disabilities: Research and future directions. *Topics in Early Childhood Special Education, 31,* 232–240. doi:10.1177/0271121411428087

Rous, B., Hallam, R., Harbin, G., McCormick, K., & Jung, L. A. (2007). The transition process for young children with disabilities: A conceptual framework. *Infants & Young Children, 20,* 135–148. doi:10.1097/01.IYC.0000264481.27947.5f

Rous, B., Hallam, R., McCormick, K., & Cox, M. (2010). Practices that support the transition to public preschool programs: Results from a national survey. *Early Childhood Research Quarterly, 25,* 17–32. doi:10.1016/j.ecresq.2009.09.001

Rous, B., Hallam, R., Turnbull, A., Buysse, V., & Winton, P., (2010). *CONNECT Module 2: Transition.* Chapel Hill: University of North Carolina, FPG Child Development Institute, CONNECT: The Center to Mobilize Early Childhood Knowledge. Retrieved from http://community.fpg.unc.edu/connect-modules/learners/module-2

Rous, B., Harbin, G., & McCormick, K. (2006, September). *A child outcome framework for the early childhood transition process* (NECTC Research Brief #2). Lexington, KY: University of Kentucky, Interdisciplinary Human Development Institute, National Early Childhood Transition Center.

Rous, B., Hemmeter, M. L., & Schuster, J. (1999). Evaluating the impact of the STEPS model on development of community-wide transition systems. *Journal of Early Intervention, 22,* 38–50. doi:10.1177/105381519902200105

Rous, B., & Mawdsley, H. (in press). Preparing teachers to support transition and bridge discontinuity for children and families. In L .J. Couse & S. L. Recchia (Eds.), *Handbook of early childhood teacher education.* New York, NY: Routledge.

Rous, B., Myers, C. T., & Stricklin, S. B. (2007). Strategies for supporting transitions of young children with special needs and their families. *Journal of Early Intervention, 30,* 1–18. doi:10.1177/105381510703000102

Schulting, A. B., Malone, P. S., & Dodge, K. A. (2005). The effect of schoolbased kindergarten transition policies and practices on child academic outcomes. *Developmental Psychology, 41,* 860–871. doi:10.1037/0012-1649.41.6.860

Shonkoff, J. P., & Phillips, D. A. (Eds.). (2000). *From neurons to neighborhoods: The science of early childhood development.* Washington, DC: National Academy Press.

11

Voices From the Field

VOICES FROM THE FIELD FEATURES PERSPECTIVES OF FAMILY MEMbers, practitioners, teachers, preservice students, administrators, researchers, professional development and higher education faculty on the revised DEC Recommended Practices.

Mindy Borden
OTR/L for the Champaign School District

Occupational therapy services have seen a shift in the manner in which they are provided. We strive to provide services within the classroom/educational setting so students have more classroom time and are able to maintain social relationships within their peer groups. These recommended practices ensure that all providers for a child are taking into account the needs of the student and his or her family. Because the family is the unit that knows and understands the child best, we as service providers should embrace that knowledge and use it to help guide and plan for a student's best interests and future.

Dana Childress
Early intervention professional development consultant for the Partnership for People with Disabilities at Virginia Commonwealth University

I consider the DEC Recommended Practices to be a specific and essential resource that provides direction for the development of meaningful training for practitioners in the field. The recommendations can and should be used to guide professional development efforts, develop competencies, strengthen training content, and facilitate assessment of learning. The efforts of the DEC Recommended Practices Committee have just made my job easier. . . . Thank you!

Lillian Durán
Associate professor at Utah State University

As faculty teaching early childhood special education classes, I have found the new DEC Recommended Practices to be an excellent resource for my methods courses. I weave them throughout my courses to provide my students with concrete information on evidence-based practices and current trends in the field. My students have also commented that they use the recommended practices as a guide for their teaching during practicum and student teaching experiences.

Erin Jackle
Instructional coach for Elgin School District

I am in a unique position to not only support our youngest learners and their teachers but to advocate for them as well. For me, the DEC Recommended Practices represent my professional "true north" as an early childhood special educator. They serve as a touch point to reflect on my own practice, a toolkit to help me support teachers to move their own practices, and a resource to move our organization forward.

Maurita Keyser
PreK/ECSE teacher at Danville School District

The DEC Recommended Practices serve as a wonderful guideline to inform my instruction and professional practice. Although my district encourages membership in organizations such as DEC, they do not fully use the resources available. The recommended practices are not something that need to be contingent on district buy-in. As an individual teacher, I can access the recommended practices and implement them independently in my classroom. The recommended practices give me something to aspire to. When I recognize that I am already doing many of these things, I gain a sense of pride and confidence in my teaching ability. The recommended practices serve as an affirmation of my skills as an educator of young children with special needs.

Heidi Meisner
PreK teacher at Urbana School District

The DEC Recommended Practices align with and complement the Illinois Early Childhood Teaching Standards for Special Education in that both push for best practice and excellence among schools, teachers, assessment, environment, and instruction. Both documents firmly advocate policies of inclusion whenever possible and encourage teachers to set realistic and achievable goals for their students that are based on evidence from observation, assessment, and reports.

Janice Myck-Wayne
Associate professor at California State University, Fullerton

As a teacher educator, I feel an immense responsibility to prepare EI/ECSE practitioners who are knowledgeable in the best practices that drive the profession. The eight domains of the DEC Recommended Practices provide a cornerstone for developing teacher candidate learning outcomes using a common language based on the most up-to-date research. I feel that the DEC Recommended Practices provide teacher candidates with a framework to guide them as they enter the profession and serve young children and their families.

Hyejin Park
Assistant professor at Arizona State University

The DEC Recommended Practices are a "must-have" resource for any teacher educator. They provide a comprehensive framework to guide teacher candidates about evidence-based practices for young children with special needs and their families. I have used them repeatedly for students' self-evaluations, program evaluations, research frameworks, and philosophy statements. They have been my companion in every step of my teaching and research work, and I know the usefulness of this book will serve my emerging teachers just the same.

Kylie Walch
Pre-K teacher at Ayeyarwaddy International School (Mandalay, Myanmar)

The DEC Recommended Practices are a wonderful "tool" to have in my "toolbox." The most useful part of these practices for me is the organization and clarity of the document. It is very clear what practices I can put into place in my classroom across the various topic strands, and the clarification of each topic strand helped make this intimidating document very understandable for me. I believe this will be a great guide for me whether my students are typically developing or have a disability. I think these practices will help me become a better teacher because I can reference this document and make informed decisions for my students and their families. These practices are also a great guide to allow me to see what I am doing in my classroom and what my next steps might be.

12

RESOURCES WITHIN REASON

Foundational Resources for Each Area of the DEC Recommended Practices

CAMILLE CATLETT
University of North Carolina at Chapel Hill

EIGHT AREAS OF PRACTICE ARE IDENTIFIED IN THE DEC RECOMMENDed Practices. This section highlights a few resources for each area that the authors and content experts have identified as foundational. Exploring each set of resources will help anyone to discover more about the fundamentals of each aspect of a recommended practice. The lists are not intended to be comprehensive. Subsequent monographs in this series will provide a more extensive set of resources for each area. All resources are free online.

Assessment

Division for Early Childhood (DEC)

Position statements from DEC (e.g., Promoting Positive Outcomes for Children With Disabilities: Recommendations for Curriculum, Assessment, and Program Evaluation; Development Delay as an Eligibility Category) offer significant contributions to thinking about how to apply the DEC Recommended Practices to aspects of the assessment process.

    https://www.dec-sped.org/papers

The Early Childhood Technical Assistance Center (ECTA)

ECTA is funded by the U.S. Department of Education's Office of Special Education Programs to improve state early intervention and early childhood special education service systems, increase the implementation of effective practices, and enhance the outcomes of these programs for young children and their families. The Early Intervention: Screening, Evaluation, and Assessment section of its website offers a variety of resources related to assessment.

> http://ectacenter.org/topics/earlyid/screeneval.asp

National Association for the Education of Young Children (NAEYC)

Position statements from NAEYC (e.g., Curriculum, Assessment, and Program Evaluation; Screening and Assessment of Young English Language Learners) offer significant contributions to thinking about how to apply the DEC Recommended Practices to aspects of the assessment process within the context of developmentally appropriate practice.

> http://www.naeyc.org/positionstatements

Technical Assistance Center on Social Emotional Intervention for Young Children (TACSEI)

The TACSEI website offers a variety of resources to support the Assessment recommended practices. These range from delineating the dos and don'ts of functional assessment to evidence-based information about functional behavioral assessment.

> http://challengingbehavior.fmhi.usf.edu/

Environment

Center on Technology and Disability (CTD) Institute

OSEP's Center on Technology and Disability (CTD) helps educators, families, and organizations to implement effective assistive and instructional technology. The CTD provides information and technical assistance on assistive and instructional technology for children and youth with disabilities. You can subscribe to receive e-mail updates about upcoming CTD events and activities.

> http://www.ctdinstitute.org/

Head Start Center for Inclusion

The goal of the Head Start Center for Inclusion is to "increase the competence, confidence, and effectiveness of personnel in Head Start programs to include children with disabilities." However, the available resources hosted on its website could be helpful for all practitioners seeking to support the access and participation of children with disabilities in inclusive classrooms.

> https://depts.washington.edu/hscenter/

Section on Pediatrics Fact Sheets and Resources

The Section on Pediatrics of the American Physical Therapy Association publishes several open access fact sheets for practitioners and consumers to promote participation for children with disabilities and their families. Fact sheet topics include natural environments, assistive technology, and fitness for young children, to name a few.

>https://pediatricapta.org/fact-sheets/

Universal Design for Learning Resources

An evidence-based practice that is underscored in the Environment recommended practices is universal design for learning (UDL). UDL is a set of principles for curriculum development to give all individuals equal opportunities to learn. Here are three articles that illustrate how UDL can be used to support young children of diverse abilities:

Bertling, J., Darrah, M., Lyon, D., & Jackson, S. (n.d.). Early childhood building blocks: Universal design for learning in early childhood inclusive classrooms. *Resources for Early Childhood: An Online Resource for Ohio's Educators.*

>http://rec.ohiorc.org/orc_documents/orc/recv2/briefs/pdf/0018.pdf

Conn-Powers, M., Frazeur Cross, A., Krider Traub, E., & Hutter-Pishgahi, L. (2006, September). The universal design of early education: Moving forward for all children. *Young Children on the Web.*

>http://journal.naeyc.org/btj/200609/ConnPowersBTJ.pdf

Dinnebeil, L. A., Boat, M., & Bae, Y. (2013). Integrating principles of universal design into the early childhood curriculum. *Dimensions of Early Childhood, 41*(1), 3–13.

>http://www.southernearlychildhood.org/upload/pdf/Dimensions_Vol41_1_Dinnebeil.pdf

Family

Beach Center on Disability

The Beach Center on Disability is a multidisciplinary research and training center committed to making a significant and sustainable positive difference in the quality of life of individuals and families affected by disability and the professionals who support them. The Families section of the website includes an array of resources (articles, research, tools, measures, networking opportunities) related to the Family recommended practices.

>http://www.beachcenter.org/families/default.aspx

The Early Childhood Technical Assistance Center (ECTA)

ECTA is funded by the Office of Special Education Programs to improve state early intervention and early childhood special education service systems, increase the implementation of effective practices, and enhance the outcomes of these programs for young children and their families. The Family-Centered

Principles and Practices section of its website offers a variety of resources that align with or are supportive of the Family recommended practices.

> http://ectacenter.org/topics/families/famctrprin.asp

Illinois Early Intervention Training Program

Visit this website to discover a Web-based repository of material related to the Family recommended practices in the Family Resources section.

> http://www.illinoiseitraining.org/page.aspx?item=116

PACER Center

The mission of PACER Center (Parent Advocacy Coalition for Educational Rights) is to expand opportunities and enhance the quality of life of children and young adults with disabilities and their families, based on the concept of parents helping parents. Click on the Resources section of the website to discover programs, publications, newsletters, policy documents, videos, and websites that can be useful in implementing the Family recommended practices.

> http://www.pacer.org/pandr/

Instruction

Center on the Social and Emotional Foundations for Early Learning (CSEFEL)

CSEFEL is focused on promoting the social emotional development and school readiness of young children from birth to age 5. Resources of all types (research, videos, modules, articles, etc.) are available on this website to support the Instruction recommended practices.

> http://csefel.vanderbilt.edu/

CONNECT Module 1: Embedded Interventions

The Instruction recommended practices underscore the importance of "embedding instruction within and across routines, activities, and environments." A multifaceted resource for building this capacity is this online module, which includes handouts, activities, videos, research, narratives, and other materials. The module also supports an evidence-based decision-making process for implementing these practices effectively.

> http://community.fpg.unc.edu/connect-modules/learners/module-1

Embedded Instruction for Early Learning

This website offers research and resources for families and professionals on embedded instruction, including information on using these practices in home and school settings.

> http://www.embeddedinstruction.net/

Embedded Learning Opportunities

This section of the Head Start Center on Inclusion website offers PowerPoints, videos, activities, modules, and other resources for supporting audiences that range from professional development providers to family members.

http://depts.washington.edu/hscenter/elo

Interaction

Center for Early Literacy Learning (CELL)

CELL has guided the development of evidence-based resources for supporting interactions. Visit the home page (http://earlyliteracylearning.org/) to access a variety of tools and resources. Two examples are provided below.

> **Classroom Responsive Teaching:** This section of the CELL website includes a self-guided module on responsive teaching that focuses on specific responsive techniques an adult can use to promote a child's exploration of literacy.
>
> http://www.earlyliteracylearning.org/responteach1c.php
>
> **Products for Practitioners:** Downloadable products, ranging from videos to practice guides, are available in this section of the website.
>
> http://www.earlyliteracylearning.org/practresource1.php

The Hanen Centre

The Tips for Parents section of this website offers helpful information for families and professionals related to supporting language and literacy.

http://www.hanen.org/Helpful-Info/Parent-Tips.aspx

Zero to Three

The Zero to Three website offers an array of resources for supporting recommended interactions among family members, caregivers, and young children. Here are a few examples:

> The **Free Parent Brochures and Guides** section offers practical resources in English and Spanish.
>
> http://www.zerotothree.org/about-us/areas-of-expertise/free-parent-brochures-and-guides/
>
> The **School Readiness Interactive Birth to 3** section is an interactive learning tool designed to help parents and caregivers encourage their young children's early learning.
>
> http://www.zerotothree.org/early-care-education/school-readiness-interactive-birth-to-3/

Leadership

DEC Position Statement on Leadership

New guidance from DEC offers insights on promoting high-quality leadership that is consistent with recommended practices at all levels of the early intervention/early childhood special education service system.

http://www.dec-sped.org/papers

Teaming and Collaboration

Kansas Inservice Training System (KITS)

KITS produces short informational briefs available for free download in PDF format, two of which focus on practices related to teaming and collaboration.

Enhancing Family Participation in the IFSP/IEP Process

http://kskits.org/ta/Packets/EnhancingFamilyPart.shtml

Using Primary Service Providers & Coaching in Early Intervention Programs

http://kskits.org/ta/Packets/UsingPrimaryService.shtml

Center for the Advanced Study for Excellence (CASE)

CASE is a research and training institute as well as an early childhood intervention program for children (birth to age 5), families, and women who are pregnant in western North Carolina. CASE investigators and staff have emphasized research, tools, and strategies that align with and support teaming and collaboration practices. Visit the CASE's Family, Infant and Preschool Program (FIPP) website to find a significant body of work on coaching practices, the primary service provider approach to teaming, and effective family-professional collaboration.

http://fipp.org/publications/

CONNECT Project Modules

The CONNECT Project has developed free online modules, each focused on a specific research-based practice to support inclusion. Two modules have particular relevance to teaming and collaboration. Module 3: Communication for Collaboration focuses on effective communication practices that can be used to promote collaboration with professionals and families in early care and education, and intervention settings. Module 4: Family-Professional Partnerships focuses on skills to build trusting family-professional partnerships when working with families of young children.

http://community.fpg.unc.edu/connect-modules/learners/module-3

http://community.fpg.unc.edu/connect-modules/learners/module-4

Videos That Illustrate Teaming and Collaboration

Through a partnership of the Iowa Department of Education, the Distance Mentoring Model at Florida State University, families, and Early ACCESS providers in Iowa, Larry Edelman produced the following video resources that are available for free download and viewing. The first two videos illustrate what family-guided routines based intervention (FGRBI) looks like during early intervention home visits and is narrated by providers and family members who reflect on a number of key strategies and themes. In the third video, a parent offers her perspective on the use of toy bags by home visitors.

A Home Visit with Kris and Kiyah: Early ACCESS special education teacher Peg joins Kiyah and her father, Kris, on a home visit. Peg supports Kris to embed opportunities for Kiyah to learn and participate in the family's everyday activities, such as getting ready for child care and taking a walk.

http://dmm.cci.fsu.edu/IADMM/videoexamples/KrisKiyah.html

A Home Visit with Brandon's Family: Early ACCESS speech-language pathologist Alison works with Brandon's parents on ways to support Brandon's language development. The family practices using new strategies during the visit and makes plans to use the strategies throughout the week.

http://dmm.cci.fsu.edu/IADMM/videoexamples/Brandon.html

Families Talk About the Toy Bag: Brandon's parents discuss the benefits of using their toys and materials for Brandon's play rather than toys brought in by an early intervention provider.

http://dmm.cci.fsu.edu/IADMM/videoexamples/ToyBag.html

Transition

CONNECT Module 2: Transition

Policy advisories, research syntheses, activities, handouts, video clips, and supports for evidence-based practice decisions are among the resources available in this multifaceted module.

http://community.fpg.unc.edu/connect-modules/learners/module-2

National Early Childhood Transition Center (NECTC)

NECTC's mission is to examine factors that promote successful transitions among infant/toddler programs, preschool programs, and public school programs for young children with disabilities and their families. The instruments, protocols, research, and ideas of the NECTC have much to offer in terms of resources to support the implementation of the Transition recommended practices.

http://www.hdi.uky.edu/nectc/NECTC/Home

Transition from Part C to Preschool

This website collects policies, guidelines, illustrations, and examples to promote effective transition practices.

http://ectacenter.org/topics/transition/transition.asp

Note: The author gratefully acknowledges the contributions of the following contributors to this section: Rashida Banerjee, Tricia Catalino, Chelsea Guillen, Lori Meyer, Jane Squires, Carol Trivette, and Pam Winton.

13

PARTICIPANTS

Contributors to Revisions of the 2014 Recommended Practices

Recommended Practices Commission for the 2014 Revision

Current Members
Mary McLean, chair
Rashida Banerjee
Judith Carta
Tricia Catalino
Chelsea Guillen
Kathleen Hebbeler
Mary Louise Hemmeter
Lori E. Meyer

Susan Sandall
Patricia Snyder
Judy Swett
Pam Winton

Past Member
Barbara Smith, past chair

Technical Advisors for Evidence Validation: Gap Analysis Group

Mary Beth Bruder
Judith Carta
Carl Dunst
Glen Dunlap
Mary Louise Hemmeter
Mary McLean
Alissa Rausch

Lori A. Roggman
Rosa Milagros Santos
Susan Sandall
Patricia Snyder
Phil Strain
Carol M. Trivette

Recommended Practices Topic Workgroup Leaders and Commission Liaisons (2014)

(TL) Topic leads
(WG) Workgroup members
(CL) Commission liaisons

Assessment
Stephen Bagnato (TL)
Jane Squires (TL)
Serra Acar (WG)
Susan Killmeyer (WG)
Sumeyye Koten-Glucu (WG)
Marisa Macy (WG)
Eileen McKeating (WG)
Lois Pribble (WG)
Alison Baker Wilson (WG)
Kathleen Hebbeler (CL)
Mary McLean (CL)

Environment
Rena Hallam (TL)
Bill Brown (WG)
Deborah Cassidy (WG)
Robyn Ridgely (WG)
Kaitlin Bargreen (WG)
Eleni Soukakou (WG)
Tricia Catalino (CL)
Lori E. Meyer (CL)

Family
Carol M. Trivette (TL)
Carl Dunst (WG)
Marilyn Espe-Sherwindt (WG)
Lori A. Roggman (WG)
Carla Peterson (WG)
Rashida Banerjee (CL)
Judy Swett (CL)

Interactional
Lise Fox (TL)
Tweety Yates (TL)
Jeanette McCollum (WG)
Judith Carta (CL)

Instructional
Ilene Schwartz (TL)
Juliann Woods (TL)
Erin Barton (WG)
Jennifer Brown (WG)
Jennifer Fung (WG)
Howard Goldstein (WG)
Eva Horn (WG)
Mary Louise Hemmeter (CL)
Patricia Snyder (CL)

Leadership
Chelsea Guillen (CL)
Kathleen Hebbeler (CL)
Barbara Smith (CL)
Pam Winton (CL)

Teaming and Collaboration
M'Lisa Shelden (TL)
Laurie Dinnebeil (WG)
Dathan Rush (WG)
Robin McWilliam (WG)
Chelsea Guillen (CL)
Pam Winton (CL)

Transition
Beth S. Rous (TL)
Helena Mawdsley (WG)
Katherine McCormick (WG)
Susan Sandall (CL)

Dual Language Learners
Rosa Milagros Santos
Lillian Durán

DEC Recommended Practices Commission Support
Betsy Ayankoya
Dale Epstein

Index

access, 58
acquisition stage in learning, 77
active learning, 79
activity, physical, 60–61
activity matrix, 83
adaptive skills, 44
administrative leaders. *See* leadership practices
adult-child interaction, 45, 88–91
advocacy, 32
Ages & Stages Questionnaires, 42
aggressive behavior, 84
alignment, 112–113
artificial activities, 39
ASD (autism spectrum disorder), 82, 92, 95
assessment, 37–50
    artificial activities in, 39
    assessment processes, 41–47
    assessment properties, 41
    authentic, 40, 42, 43, 44, 46
    challenges in, 38–39
    defined, 37
    developmentally appropriate, 40
    empirical support for, 47–49
    federal requirements for, 37
    mismeasurement in, 39
    naturalistic, 40, 43, 44–45, 47, 48
    parental involvement in, 48
    positive focus in, 39
    purpose of, 37–38
    refining assessment practices, 50
    resources for, 125–126
assessment systems, 41, 43
assistive technology (AT), 59–60
authentic assessments, 40, 42, 43, 44, 46. *See also* naturalistic assessments
autism spectrum disorder (ASD), 82, 92, 95
Ayankoya, Betsy, 14–15

Banerjee, Rashida, 15
Bargreen, Kaitlin, 54
Battelle Developmental Inventory, 44, 48–49
Bayley Scales of Infant Development, 44, 48–49
behavior challenges in assessment, 39
behavioral rating scales, 47
best vs. recommended practices, 2
blindness, 55, 92, 93
Brief Infant Toddler Social Emotional Assessment, 42
Brigance Early Childhood Screens, 42
Brown, Bill, 54

caregiver-child interaction, 45, 88–91
Carta, Judith, 12, 14
Cassidy, Deborah, 54
Catalino, Tricia, 15
CBMs (curriculum-based measures), 42, 44, 49
center-based meetings, 65, 71–72
cerebral palsy, 92
Child Behavior Checklist, 46
Child Find, 37
child transition profiles, 116
child-adult interaction, 45, 88–91
classroom visits, 115, 116, 117
coaching, 81
cognitive delay, 47–48
collaboration, 30–32, 59, 68, 101, 102. *See also* teaming and collaboration practices
collaborative teaming, 100
collective responsibility and teamwork, 99
commission, 6, 14–23, 33, 54, 59, 100, 133–134
commission liaisons, 134
communication, 44–45, 80–81, 84, 87–91, 96, 102–105, 115–117. *See also* interaction practices
communication evaluations, 38
contingent responsiveness, 91
continuity, 112–113
coordination, 102
curriculum-based measures (CBMs), 42, 44, 49

DAPs (developmentally appropriate practices), 54–55
DEC (Division for Early Childhood), 1–2
DEC Conference (1991), 2
DEC Conference (1998), 4
DEC Conference (2012), 14–15
DEC Conference (2013), 21
DEC Executive Board, 1, 2, 12–13, 15, 21, 23, 54
DEC Executive Committee, 2
DEC Recommended Practices (1993), 1–3
DEC Recommended Practices (2000), 3–6
DEC Recommended Practices (2005 guide), 5–6, 54, 99–100
DEC Recommended Practices (2014). *See also* history of DEC Recommended Practices
    action plan for, 18
    definitions for, 16
    evidence validation of, 21–22
    feedback from the field, 121–123
    framework for, 16
    implementation of, 22–23
    input gathering for, 19–21
    iterative processes for, 18–19
    parameters for, 15, 16–17
    terms used in, 17
    topic areas for, 16
    workgroups for developing, 12–13, 18–19, 21–22, 54, 134
DEC Recommended Practices Commission, 6, 14–23, 33, 54, 59, 100, 133–134
DEC Recommended Practices Task Force, 1, 2–3, 6
DEC Recommended Practices timeline, 6
DEC Recommended Practices Workbook, 6
decontextualized settings, 83
developmental challenges in assessment, 39
developmental psychology, 39
developmental screening, 42–43
developmentally appropriate assessment, 40
developmentally appropriate practices (DAPs), 54–55
direct practices, 33
distal environmental factors, 56
Division for Early Childhood (DEC). *See* DEC (Division for Early Childhood)
domain specific tests, 42
Down syndrome, 47, 92, 105–106

early childhood special education (ECSE), 3, 25–29
Early Childhood Technical Assistance Center (ECTA), 13–15, 18–23
Early Intervention SIG, 73
early intervention/early childhood special education (EI/ECSE) system, 3, 25–29
Early Screening Inventory, 42
ecological theory of human development, 53
ECSE (early childhood special education), 3, 25–29
ECTA (Early Childhood Technical Assistance Center), 13–15, 18–23
educational planning, 42, 44
EI/ECSE (early intervention/early childhood special education) system, 3, 25–29
eligibility/diagnostic assessment, 42, 43–47. *See also* assessment
embedded instruction, 79–85
embedded intervention, 81
environment practices, 53–62
    access and, 58

assistive technology (AT) and, 60
collaboration in changing environments, 59
conceptualizing environments, 55–56
DAPs and, 54–55
enhancing capacity of environment, 58–59, 61–62
environmental factors, 56
environmental features, 55–58, 60, 61
environmental settings, 55, 56, 58, 79
evolution of, 54
fitness and wellness and, 60–61
key ideas of, 57–59
participation and, 58
resources for, 126–127
workgroup for, 54
Epstein, Dale, 14–15
evaluation, 42, 44
evidence validation technical advisors, 133. *See also* Gap Analysis Group
evidence-based practice, 11
executive board, 1, 2, 12–13, 15, 21, 23, 54
executive committee, 2

facilitative management, 29
family, definition of, 66
family characteristics, 67
family practices, 65–73
    center-based meetings in, 65, 71–72
    home-based meetings in, 65, 70–71
    implementation procedures, 70–72
    practitioner support in, 73
    principles of, 66–68
    purpose of, 66, 69–70
    research evidence of, 68–69
    resources for, 127–128
family-centered practices, 67
fine-motor delays, 55
fitness and wellness, 60–61
fluency stage in learning, 77
focus groups, 4–5, 9
Fowler, Susan, 2
functional behavior assessment (FBA), 46, 84
functional communication training, 84

Gap Analysis Group, 19, 21–22, 23, 103, 133
generalization stage in learning, 77
gross-motor delays, 44, 55

group facilitation strategies, 102, 104
Guillen, Chelsea, 15

Hallam, Rena, 54
Hebbeler, Kathleen, 12, 14
Hemmeter, Mary Louise, 14
history of DEC Recommended Practices, 1–23. *See also* DEC Recommended Practices (2014)
    1993 recommended practices, 1–3
    2000 recommended practices, 3–6
    2005 recommended practices guide, 5–6, 54, 99–100
    2014 recommended practices, 12–23
    DEC commission, role of, 6, 14–23, 33, 54, 59, 100, 133–134
    DEC conferences and, 2, 4, 13, 14–15, 21
    DEC Recommended Practices Workbook published, 6
    ECTA and, 13–15, 18–23
    focus groups, role of, 4–5, 9
    interdisciplinary practices and, 99–100
    stakeholder input in developing practices, 4, 5, 13, 14, 19–20
    timeline, 6
    workgroups, role of, 2, 12–13, 18–19, 21–22, 54, 134
home visits, 81, 82, 84, 102, 116, 117
home-based meetings, 65, 70–71

ICF (International Classification of Functioning and Health), 58
IDEA (Individuals With Disabilities Education Act, 2004), 26–27, 37, 60, 100
imitative turn-taking, 94
inactivity, 61
inclusion, 30–31, 100
Inclusion SIG, 73
inclusive classrooms, 83
inclusive environments, 55, 56, 58, 79
indirect support practices, 9, 32–33
Individuals With Disabilities Education Act, 2004 (IDEA), 26–27, 37, 60, 100
information sharing, 104–105
infrastructure, 27
instruction, definition of, 77
instruction, embedded, 79–85

instruction practices, 77–85
    activity matrix in, 83
    case studies in, 78–85
    coaching in, 81
    core components, 85
    decontextualized settings defined, 83
    defined, 16, 77–78
    embedded instruction, 79–85
    embedded settings defined, 83–84
    functional communication training in, 84
    instruction defined, 77
    learning process and, 77
    purpose of, 77
    resources for, 128–129
    strategies in, 78
    visual supports in, 83
interaction practices, 87–96. *See also* communication
    adult-child interaction in, 88–91
    child development and learning and, 91
    described, 87–88
    disruption and, 92
    individual differences and, 92–95
    influences on quality of, 92
    intervention and, 92–94
    reciprocal interaction, 88–91
    resources for, 129
    responsive interaction, 91–96
interconnection of recommended practices, 57–58
interdisciplinary teams, 101
International Classification of Functioning and Health (ICF), 58
intervention, embedded, 81
interviews, 47

Johnson, Larry, 2

Keilty, Bonnie, 13
kindergarten assessments, 46

leaders, 25, 28–29, 33
leadership practices, 25–33
    administrative leaders described, 25–28
    collaboration and advocacy in, 30–32
    EI/ECSE system and, 25–29
    facilitative management in, 29
    implementing, 29–30, 33
    leadership defined, 25, 28–29, 33
    managing defined, 28
    personal practices and, 32
    practitioner/child/family interaction and, 26
    previous recommended practices and, 32–33
    purpose of, 28
    resources for, 130
    visionary management and, 29–30
learning process, 77
legal foundation for service provision, 1–2, 26–27
Likert scale, 46
linked assessment, 41, 43, 48, 49
literature reviews, 68–69

MacArthur-Bates Communicative Development Inventory, 42
maintenance stage in learning, 77
managing, definition of, 28
McEvoy, Mary, 2
McLean, Mary, 2, 4, 14
meta-analytic reviews, 68–69
Meyer, Lori E., 15
mismeasurement, 39
Mulligan, Sarah, 12
multidisciplinary teams, 101

natural environments, 55, 56, 58
naturalistic assessments, 40, 43, 44–45, 47, 48. *See also* authentic assessments
norm-referenced tests, 42, 43–44, 47

observational instruments, 45–46
Odom, Sam, 2, 4

parent capacity-building practices, 67–68
parental role in family practices, 66–67
parent-implemented communication interventions, 81
parent-mediated intervention, 93
parent-professional collaborative partnerships, 68
participation, 58
Peabody Developmental Motor Scales, 42
Perrett, Susie, 2
phase in days, 116
physical activity, 60–61
physical environment, 55, 57, 58, 60, 61
physical impairments, 60

PICCOLO checklist, 45
portfolio assessments, 46
practices, definition of, 11, 17, 66
practitioner-child-family interaction, 26
practitioner-parent collaborative partnerships, 68
practitioners, 17, 33, 66, 73, 114
preschool-age children, 38–39
Pretti-Frontczak, Kristie, 13
primary service provider (PSP), 101, 105–106
problem solving in teams, 103
professional standards, 31–32
proximal environmental factors, 56
Public Law 99-457, 1–2

rating scales, 46–47
reciprocal interactions, 88–91
Recommended Practices. *See* DEC Recommended Practices
Recommended Practices Commission, 6, 14–23, 33, 54, 59, 100, 133–134
recommended practices criteria, 11
recommended vs. best practices, 2
reliability, 41
research study reviews, 68–69
research-based practices, 17
resources, 125–132
responsive interaction, 91–96
revising recommended practices. *See* DEC Recommended Practices (2014)
Ridgely, Robyn, 54

Salisbury, Chris, 2
Sandall, Susan, 4, 14
Santos, Rosa Milagros, 12, 13
screening, 31, 41–43
self-care, 32
self-efficacy, 68
self-initiated movement, 61
Senate Bill 2294 (1986), 1
sensory function tests, 42
Sexton, David, 4
SIGs (special interest groups), 73
Smith, Barbara, 2, 4, 14, 15
Snyder, Patricia, 4, 12, 14
social environment, 55, 57, 58
social skills, 44
social-emotional/behavioral assessments, 42, 47

sociocultural competence, 41
Soukakou, Eleni, 54
special interest groups (SIGs), 73
spina bifida, 78
standardized assessments, 48–49
standardized norm-referenced tests, 42, 43–44, 47
standards, 31–32
state competencies, 31
Stayton, Vicki, 2
Strain, Phil, 4
strands and strand chairs, 2, 3, 4, 9
strengths-based perspective, 59
Swett, Judy, 15
systematic literature reviews, 68–69

task force, 1, 2–3, 6
teaming and collaboration practices, 99–106
    background, 99–100
    collaboration defined, 101, 102
    coordination defined, 102
    factors influencing, 102
    inclusion and, 100
    practices and examples, 102–106
    primary service provider approach in, 105–106
    principles of, 100–102
    rationale for, 100
    resources for, 130–131
    team capacity building and, 103
    team composition and, 102
    team defined, 101
    team planning and implementation in, 103
    team purpose, 102
    teaming terminology, 100–102
teams, 101–103
Technical Advisors for Evidence Validation: Gap Analysis Group, 133
temporal environment, 55, 57
Thomas, Daphne, 2
Thompson, Bruce, 4
timeline for DEC Recommended Practices, 6
topic workgroup leaders, 134
topic workgroups, 18–19, 21–22, 54, 134
transdisciplinary principle, 99
transdisciplinary teams, 101
transition, definition of, 112
transition plans, 116

transition practices, 111–118
    changing context of early childhood education and, 111
    communication between practitioners during transition, 115–117
    components of transition planning, 112–113
    impact on adjustment and outcomes, 115
    implementing, 113
    planned and timely strategies in, 116–118
    practitioner role in, 114
    resources for, 131–132
    timing in transition process, 113–114
    transition defined, 112
transition profiles, 116

Trivette, Carol M., 13
turn-taking interactions, 89–90

utility, 41

validity, 41
Vineland Adaptive Behavior Scale, 47
visionary management, 29–30
visual impairment, 55, 92, 93
visual supports for learning, 83

Winton, Pam, 15
workgroup leaders, 134
workgroups, 2, 12–13, 18–19, 21–22, 54, 134

Illinois Early Learning Project

Connect to the world of early learning in Illinois at http://illinoisearlylearning.org
or http://illinoisearlylearning.org/index-sp.htm (in Spanish)

- Informative "Tip Sheets" in English, Spanish, Polish, Korean, and Chinese on early learning and development.
- Resources to help implement the Illinois Early Learning and Development Standards.
- Resources to help implement the Illinois Early Learning Guidelines for Infants and Toddlers.
- Los recursos de IEL están disponibles también en español.

 http://iecam.illinois.edu

IECAM provides a comprehensive picture of early care and education services in Illinois by combining...

Demographic Data
- population
- poverty level
- language use

Early Childhood Program Data
- state agencies
- Head Start/Early Head Start
- child care

IECAM users can see — in tables or maps — the distribution of early childhood services in counties, townships, legislative districts, and/or municipalities.

http://eiclearinghouse.org
Best-practice information on addressing developmental delays in young children. Visit our website to access:
- recommended resources
- free lending library of books & DVDs
- family experiences and handouts

Newsletters – Resource Lists – Parent Stories – Podcasts – Resources in Spanish

Division for Early Childhood's 32nd Annual International Conference on Young Children with Special Needs and their Families

Galt House Hotel
140 North 4th Street, Louisville, KY 40202

For additional information
www.dec-sped.org/conference ★ conference@dec-sped.org ★ 310-428-7209

13th ANNUAL Young Child EXPO & CONFERENCE

APRIL 13–15, 2016
WYNDHAM NEW YORKER HOTEL

Great Speakers. Great Learning. Helping Young Children Learn & Grow

- Over 100 Speakers
- Over 80 Presentations
- Full Day Pre-Conference Workshop
- 40 Exhibitors
- 1500 Attendees

Great training for all professionals working with all young children (typically developing & autism/special needs) including Teachers, Special Ed Teachers, Psychologists, SW, Speech, OT, PT, ABA, Program Directors/Principals/Administrators, Pediatricians, and Child Care Professionals.

To register go to: www.YoungChildExpo.com
or call 212-787-9700, ext. 333
Early Bird & Group Discounts Available

Presented by
losniños SERVICES

WKU's MAE in Interdisciplinary Early Childhood Education is ranked #5 in SuperScholar's Top 50 Online Graduate Programs

WKU offers both undergraduate and graduate programs in Interdisciplinary Early Childhood Education

Career Options:
- kindergarten teacher
- preschool teacher
- early childhood special educator (age 0-5 years)
- developmental interventionist
- infant-toddler teacher
- early childhood parent educator
- special educator for IEP's and IFSP's
- home-based early childhood teacher
- itinerant early childhood teacher
- nursery school teacher

For more information:
http://www.wku.edu/ste/iece
270-745-3135
margaret.gichuru@wku.edu

WKU COLLEGE OF EDUCATION & BEHAVIORAL SCIENCES

A world in which children of all abilities learn, play, and grow together.

haring center

The Haring Center strives to improve the lives of children with developmental disabilities and their families through the creation of inclusive communities.

Conducting research and training to promote inclusive education

Visit haringcenter.org to learn more.

W

Focus on Abilities!

DEVELOPMENTAL THERAPY INSTITUTE, INC.

Proven practices for early childhood since 1978.

www.developmentaltherapyinstitute.org

IMPLEMENT BEST PRACTICES
with must-have books and tools from
BROOKES

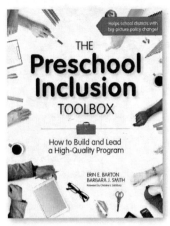
Make inclusion a reality through big-picture, systems-level change

Learn the nuts and bolts of ABI for children birth to 5

Introductory text aligned with DEC recommended practices

Master effective early intervention practices

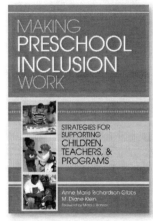
Reliable supports and strategies for future inclusive educators

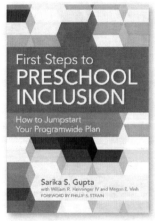
Launch a successful inclusive early childhood program

SCREENING & ASSESSMENT TOOLS

Assess the quality of parent–child interactions

The trusted developmental and social-emotional screeners

Assessment, intervention, & programming for children birth to 6

A tool for assessing and monitoring social-emotional development in young children at risk for delays

Measure teachers' implementation of the *Pyramid Model for Promoting Social Emotional Competence in Infants and Young Children.*

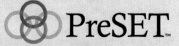
Your comprehensive tool for assessing program-wide PBIS

 www.brookespublishing.com | 1-800-638-3775 | CONNECT WITH US: